1

Reading for a Reason
Expanding Reading Skills

Laurie Blass
Elizabeth Whalley

Reading for a Reason Student Book 1: Expanding Reading Skills

ISBN 0-07-294211-8
 2 3 4 5 6 7 8 9 CCW/PCR 11 10 09 08 07 06

Editorial director: Tina Carver
Executive editor: Erik Gundersen
Development editor: Linda O'Roke
Production manager: MaryRose Malley
Interior designer: Monotype Composition
Cover designer: Monotype Composition
Photo researchers: David Mcfarlane, David Averbach

The **McGraw·Hill** Companies

Acknowledgements

The publisher and authors would like to thank the following educational professionals whose comments, reviews, and assistance were instrumental in the development of *Reading for a Reason 1: Expanding Reading Skills*.

- ▶ Fairlie Atkinson, Sungkyunkwan University, Seoul, Korea

- ▶ Lynne Barsky, Suffolk County Community College, Jericho, NY

- ▶ Gerry Boyd, Northern Virginia Community College, Annandale, VA

- ▶ Donna Fujimoto, Osaka Jogakuin Daigaku, Osaka, Japan

- ▶ Ann-Marie Hadzima, National Taiwan University, Taipei, Taiwan, R.O.C.

- ▶ Patricia Heiser, University of Washington, Seattle, WA

- ▶ Yu-shen Hsu, Soochow University, Taipei, Taiwan, R.O.C.

- ▶ Greg Keech, City College of San Francisco, San Francisco, CA

- ▶ Irene Maksymjuk, Boston University, Boston, MA

- ▶ Yoshiko Matsubayashi, Kokusai Junior College, Tokyo, Japan

- ▶ Lorraine Smith, Adelphi University, Garden City, NY

- ▶ Leslie Eloise Somers, Miami-Dade County Public Schools, Miami, FL

- ▶ Karen Stanley, Central Piedmont Community College, Charlotte, NC

This book is dedicated to Tamera Lerman.

Heartfelt thanks to the McGraw-Hill team, especially Erik Gundersen and Linda O'Roke, who helped shape this series and enhanced our enjoyment of the process.

The authors would like to thank all at the Plant, with special thanks to Frank and Gray for help with Chapter 5 and the public libraries of Palo Alto, California, and Menlo Park, California.

Table of Contents

Welcome to Reading for a Reason

Reading for a Reason 1 is the first in a three-level reading series that leads students to develop the critical reading and vocabulary skills they need to become confident, academic readers.

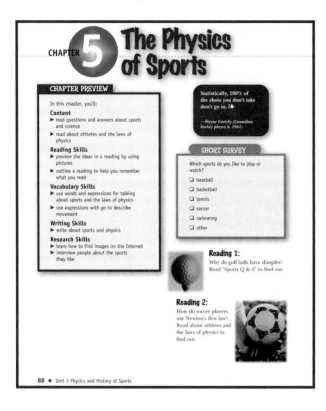

Chapter Preview boxes outline the main goals of the chapter and focus students' attention on what they will learn.

Short Surveys related to the chapter topic help students personalize the chapter content and activate prior knowledge.

Teaser photographs and questions pique students' interest.

Before You Read activities stimulate background knowledge, focus on vocabulary presentation and practice, and introduce important expressions.

Preview questions activate schemata and help students focus on the main idea of the passage.

Vocabulary Exercises preview the important words and expressions found in the readings.

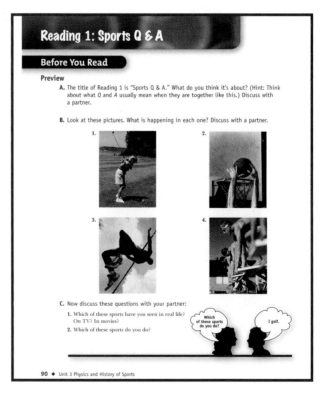

As You Read activities present readings that recycle reading skills and vocabulary to build reading fluency and confidence, while increasing mastery.

Focus questions help students focus while reading and reinforce prediction skills.

First reading passage introduces the chapter topic in a short informal reading. Types of texts include emails, interviews, quizzes, and magazine articles.

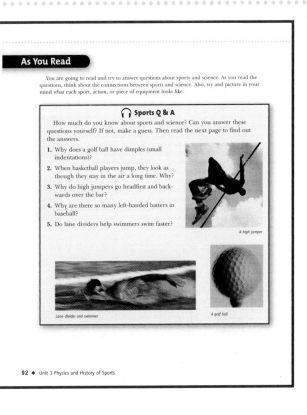

As You Read

You are going to read and try to answer questions about sports and science. As you read the questions, think about the connections between sports and science. Also, try and picture in your mind what each sport, action, or piece of equipment looks like.

🎧 Sports Q & A

How much do you know about sports and science? Can you answer these questions yourself? If not, make a guess. Then read the next page to find out the answers.

1. Why does a golf ball have dimples (small indentations)?
2. When basketball players jump, they look as though they stay in the air a long time. Why?
3. Why do high jumpers go headfirst and backwards over the bar?
4. Why are there so many left-handed batters in baseball?
5. Do lane dividers help swimmers swim faster?

A high jumper

Lane divider and swimmer

A golf ball

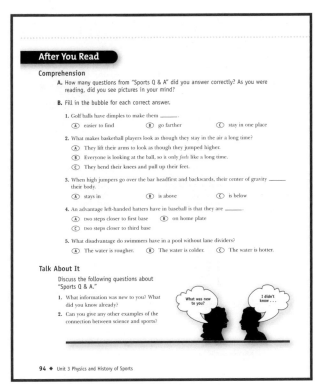

After You Read

Comprehension

A. How many questions from "Sports Q & A" did you answer correctly? As you were reading, did you see pictures in your mind?

B. Fill in the bubble for each correct answer.

1. Golf balls have dimples to make them _____.
   Ⓐ easier to find   Ⓑ go farther   Ⓒ stay in one place

2. What makes basketball players look as though they stay in the air a long time?
   Ⓐ They lift their arms to look as though they jumped higher.
   Ⓑ Everyone is looking at the ball, so it only *feels* like a long time.
   Ⓒ They bend their knees and pull up their feet.

3. When high jumpers go over the bar headfirst and backwards, their center of gravity _____ their body.
   Ⓐ stays in   Ⓑ is above   Ⓒ is below

4. An advantage left-handed batters have in baseball is that they are _____.
   Ⓐ two steps closer to first base   Ⓑ on home plate
   Ⓒ two steps closer to third base

5. What disadvantage do swimmers have in a pool without lane dividers?
   Ⓐ The water is rougher.   Ⓑ The water is colder.   Ⓒ The water is hotter.

Talk About It

Discuss the following questions about "Sports Q & A."

1. What information was new to you? What did you know already?
2. Can you give any other examples of the connection between science and sports?

What was new to you?

I didn't know . . .

After You Read activities focus on the main idea and details presented in Reading 1.

Standardized testing formats help students become familiar with a variety of test formats.

Talk About It activities encourage discussions on questions that help students synthesize, personalize, and extend concepts in the reading.

Second reading passage introduces a longer academic, scientific, or formal reading on the chapter topic.

Focus questions help students focus while reading, and enforce and reinforce prediction skills.

Headings, photographs, maps, and charts in the readings help students practice academic reading skills previously taught.

Timed Readings help students become aware of and improve their reading speed. Students chart their reading times in the Timed Reading Chart in the back of the book.

After You Read activities include extended vocabulary practice, reading skills presentation and practice, and collocation practice.

Main Idea questions allow students to check predictions made before the reading.

Reading Skills boxes present reading comprehension skills needed to succeed in an academic environment.

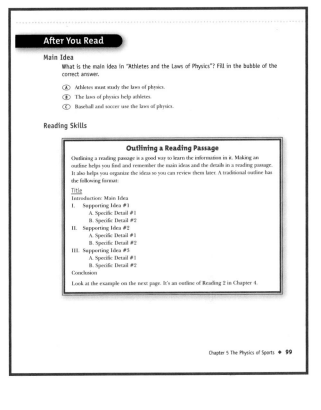

Vocabulary activities provide students with an opportunity to practice additional words and expressions from Reading 2.

Talk About It activities encourage discussions on questions that help students synthesize, personalize, and extend concepts in the reading.

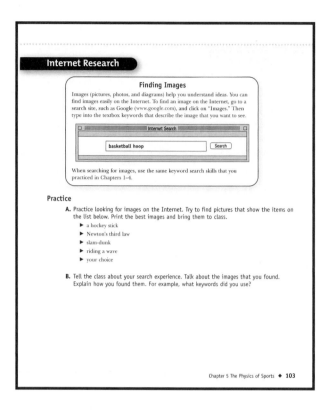

Internet Research

Finding Images

Images (pictures, photos, and diagrams) help you understand ideas. You can find images easily on the Internet. To find an image on the Internet, go to a search site, such as Google (www.google.com), and click on "Images." Then type into the textbox keywords that describe the image that you want to see.

Internet Search
basketball hoop [Search]

When searching for images, use the same keyword search skills that you practiced in Chapters 1–4.

Practice

A. Practice looking for images on the Internet. Try to find pictures that show the items on the list below. Print the best images and bring them to class.
- a hockey stick
- Newton's third law
- slam-dunk
- riding a wave
- your choice

B. Tell the class about your search experience. Talk about the images that you found. Explain how you found them. For example, what keywords did you use?

Chapter 5 The Physics of Sports ◆ **103**

Internet Research boxes present helpful tips on how to conduct academic research on the Internet.

Write About It

A. Write paragraphs. Fill in the blanks. Write complete sentences.

Paragraph One

I like to watch/play _____
[Circle one]   [Write the name of a sport]

because _____
[Explain the reason]

I also like to watch/play _____
[Circle one]   [Write the name of a sport]

because _____
[Explain the reason]

Paragraph Two

Newton's laws of physics help in many sports. One example is _____ .
[Write a sport]

Newton's _____ law helps players in this sport because
[Write the number of the law]

_____
[Explain how the law helps players]

Newton's laws also help in _____ . Newton's _____ law
[Write a sport]   [Write the number of the law]

helps players in this sport because _____
[Explain how the law helps players]

B. Now write your own paragraphs. First, write a paragraph about watching or playing sports. Then write another about how the laws of physics help in sports. Try to include four new words or expressions from this chapter.

C. Write more paragraphs about sports and science. Here are some ideas:
- Answer these questions: How can you get better at a sport that you like? What can you do? Can the laws of physics help you get better?
- Explain why you *don't* like to watch or play certain sports.
- Find an image on the Internet that shows an athlete using one of Newton's laws. Write about the law being used and how the athlete is using it.

Include four new words or expressions from this chapter in your paragraphs. Also, try to use your Internet research.

104 ◆ Unit 3 Physics and History of Sports

Write About It activities allow students to write on different but related aspects of the chapter topic.

Writing A consists of two highly structured paragraph templates to provide guided writing experience.

Writing B allows students to write two paragraphs on the same topic as Writing A.

Writing C is an open-ended writing activity.

On Your Own is a structured speaking activity that helps students further explore each chapter theme.

Step 1 has students design a survey or prepare a presentation on the chapter topic.

Step 2 asks students to conduct surveys using the questions they wrote in Step 1 or give their presentation to the class.

Step 3 allows students to explain the results of their survey or evaluate their presentations.

On Your Own

Project

Design a survey. Ask your classmates about their favorite sports.

Step 1: Practice

With a partner, design a survey about sports. Think of three questions. Write your questions in the survey box below. Have your teacher check them to make sure that they are correct. Repeat the questions with your teacher so you can pronounce them correctly.

Sports Survey

1. Question: _____
   Person 1   M _____   F _____ Answer: _____
   Person 2   M _____   F _____ Answer: _____
   Person 3   M _____   F _____ Answer: _____
2. Question: _____
   Person 1   Answer: _____
   Person 2   Answer: _____
   Person 3   Answer: _____
3. Question: _____
   Person 1   Answer: _____
   Person 2   Answer: _____
   Person 3   Answer: _____

Step 2: Take a Survey

Ask three classmates questions about sports. Indicate *M* (male) or *F* (female) for each person. Use the form above.

Step 3: Follow-Up

Explain the results of your survey to the class. For example, you could say, "I asked three people about the sports they play. Two people said that they don't play *any* sports. I was surprised because...."

Chapter 5 The Physics of Sports ◆ 105

Wrap Up

How Much Do You Remember?

Check your knowledge. In this chapter, you learned facts, words, and expressions. You also learned reading skills and you practiced writing. Complete the following to check what you remember.

1. Why do golf balls have dimples?
   _____

2. Why do basketball players look as though they stay in the air a long time?
   _____

3. What is one of Newton's laws?
   _____

4. Use *go higher than* in a sentence.
   _____

5. How do you find images on the Internet?
   _____

6. Write one thing that you learned about your classmates from your survey.
   _____

Second Timed Readings

Now reread "Sports Q & A" and "Athletes and the Laws of Physics." Time each reading separately. Write the times for all the Timed Readings in this chapter in the Timed Reading Chart on page 214.

106 ◆ Unit 3 Physics and History of Sports

Wrap Up is an informal assessment tool that reviews chapter content, vocabulary, and reading skills.

Second Timed Reading focuses students' attention on their reading fluency by having them reread Reading 1 and Reading 2 and keep track of their times on the Timed Reading Chart in the back of the book.

Scope and Sequence

Vocabulary Skills	Writing Skills	Internet and Research Skills
▶ Using words and expressions to describe friends and friendship ▶ Using comparison expressions	▶ Writing about friends, friendship, and activities with friends	▶ Using keywords to do an Internet search ▶ Interviewing people about their friends
▶ Using words and expressions to talk about love and romance ▶ Using words and expressions to discuss research	▶ Writing about love and romance	▶ Limiting Internet search results ▶ Interviewing people about their ideal mates
▶ Using words and expressions to talk about food ▶ Using verb + preposition combinations	▶ Writing about food	▶ Using an online food dictionary ▶ Interviewing people about food and eating
▶ Using words and expressions to discuss health problems ▶ Using expressions to discuss health benefits and to give advice	▶ Writing about healthy foods and eating habits	▶ Identifying valid sources of information on the Internet ▶ Interviewing people about their opinions of traditional and modern medicine
▶ Using words and expressions to discuss sports and the laws of physics ▶ Using expressions with *go* to describe movement	▶ Writing about sports and physics	▶ Finding images on the Internet ▶ Interviewing people about the sports they like
▶ Using words and expressions to talk about the history of sports ▶ Using expressions of age and time	▶ Writing about sports and sports inventions	▶ Finding biographies on the Internet ▶ Interviewing people about their sports histories

Scope and Sequence

Vocabulary Skills	Writing Skills	Internet and Research Skills
▶ Using words and expressions to talk about nature and nurture ▶ Using words and expressions to describe characteristics	▶ Writing about nature and nurture	▶ Finding recent news on the Internet ▶ Interviewing people about their opinions of nature vs. nurture
▶ Using words and expressions to discuss size and lifespan ▶ Using words to discuss extreme environments ▶ Using words and expressions to discuss animal behavior	▶ Writing about animals, longevity, and adaptation	▶ Using an online science dictionary ▶ Getting information on an animal that lives in an extreme environment
▶ Using words and expressions to talk about urban legends and storytelling ▶ Using verb + preposition combinations	▶ Writing about storytelling and urban legends	▶ Combining keywords to find specific urban legends on the Internet ▶ Interviewing people about telling jokes, stories, and urban legends
▶ Using poetic words and expressions ▶ Using words to describe poetry ▶ Using verb + *from* and *to* expressions	▶ Comparing poems and writing a poem	▶ Finding poems and information on poets on the Internet ▶ Interviewing people about their favorite poems

To the Teacher

Series Overview

Reading for a Reason: Expanding Reading Skills is a three-level academic theme-based reading series that focuses on cross-curricular content and promotes critical thinking skills. The series is designed to enhance the academic reading and vocabulary skills of English language learners. The three books in the series range from High-Beginning to High-Intermediate.

▶ Reading for a Reason 1—High-Beginning
  Reading passage word count 150–600

▶ Reading for a Reason 2—Intermediate
  Reading passage word count 425–950

▶ Reading for a Reason 3—High-Intermediate
  Reading passage word count 550–1500

The objectives of *Reading for a Reason* are to increase students' independence, confidence, competence, and comfort in reading in English and in learning new vocabulary. To be successful academically, students must have strong reading, vocabulary, and computer skills. *Reading for a Reason* is designed to work on the skills that are most needed for academic success.

To be independent readers, students need to be able to self-activate schemata and use critical thinking skills. Therefore, each book in the series promotes critical thinking skills before, during, and after the readings. The critical thinking skills include annotating a text, analyzing graphics, and identifying fact and opinion. The readings encompass a wide range of academic disciplines: biology, cultural anthropology, history, psychology, science, and sociology. Chapters recycle reading skills (such as using titles, headings, and captions to predict) taught in previous chapters. Thus, students not only have opportunities to practice skills when they are taught, but they are given additional practice in later chapters using new academic content. Students are also able to self-monitor their reading speed by filling in the chart of timed readings. Intrinsically interesting content keeps students' attention as they develop their vocabulary and reading power.

Organization of the Book

Reading for a Reason 1 is a high-beginning level book that prepares students for the academic reading they will have to do once they have begun their academic coursework. *Reading for a Reason 1* features five units that span a variety of academic disciplines. Each unit begins with an introduction to the academic discipline including a definition and explanation, a list of important people in the field, and key questions students answer to discover if they are attracted to the discipline. Each unit then consists of two twenty-page chapters that integrate reading content with reading, vocabulary, speaking, writing, and Internet research skills.

Each chapter has the following components:

- ▶ **What do you think?** presents interactive pair activities that personalize the chapter topic in more depth.

- ▶ **Before You Read** stimulates background knowledge, focuses on vocabulary presentation and practice, and introduces important expressions.

- ▶ **Reading 1** introduces the chapter topic in a short informal reading. Types of texts include emails, interviews, quizzes, and magazine articles.

- ▶ **Reading 2** introduces a longer, academic, scientific, or formal reading on the chapter topic.

- ▶ **Timed Reading** helps students become aware of and improve their reading speed by timing themselves and charting their times on the Timed Reading Chart in the back of the book.

- ▶ **Reading Skills** box presents reading comprehension skills needed to succeed in an academic environment.

- ▶ **After You Read** includes extended vocabulary practice, reading skills presentation and practice, as well as practice with collocations.

- ▶ **Talk About It** permits group discussions on questions that help students synthesize, personalize, and extend concepts in the reading.

- ▶ **Expressions** present collocations from Reading 1 and Reading 2. Practice exercises follow each box.

- ▶ **Internet Research** presents helpful tips on how to conduct academic research on the Internet. Practice exercises follow each box.

- ▶ **Write About It** allows students to write at least three different paragraphs on aspects related to the chapter topic.

- ▶ **On Your Own** presents structured speaking activities that help students further explore each chapter theme.

- ▶ **Wrap Up** is an informal assessment tool that reviews chapter content, collocations, and reading skills.

- ▶ **Crossword Puzzle** reviews vocabulary defined in the chapter.

Audio Program

Each *Reading for a Reason* book is paired with an audio program available on both audio CD and audiocassette. The audio program allows students to listen to the 20 reading passages as they read. Research shows that different students learn in different ways. By allowing students aural input, the audio program strengthens the skill sets of auditory learners. The audio program also facilitates pronunciation of individual words as well as stress, intonation, and other suprasegmentals associated with collocations. Studies have also shown that listening to readings can help increase reading speed.

Teacher Manuals

Each book in the series also has a Teacher's Manual that contains a complete answer key to the student book and chapter quizzes. The chapter quizzes consist of an additional reading passage on the chapter topic, five comprehension questions that reinforce the reading skills taught within the chapter, and five vocabulary questions. Quizzes can be photocopied and given to students for either review or assessment.

Think About Your Reading Skills

Think about your reading skills. Read the following statements and check (✔) the words that best describe you.

Before I begin a reading passage, I . . .	Never	Sometimes	Always
think about my personal connection to the topic.	_____	_____	_____
ask myself questions about the title.	_____	_____	_____
read the headings and subheadings.	_____	_____	_____
look at photos, charts, or tables and read their captions.	_____	_____	_____
read and think about the introduction.	_____	_____	_____
read the topic sentences of all the paragraphs.	_____	_____	_____

As I read a passage, I . . .	Never	Sometimes	Always
identify the main idea.	_____	_____	_____
identify details.	_____	_____	_____
identify examples.	_____	_____	_____
identify facts and opinions.	_____	_____	_____
take notes in the margin.	_____	_____	_____
guess the meanings of new words by using their contexts (the words around them).	_____	_____	_____

After I read a passage, I . . .	Never	Sometimes	Always
make a summary of it.	_____	_____	_____
predict questions about it that might be on a test.	_____	_____	_____
read it again.	_____	_____	_____

Skilled readers try to use the reading skills above as much as possible. If you don't, try to practice these skills **before, as,** and **after** you read.

What is Psychology?

Psychology is the study of people. Psychologists study how people think and how they act. They are interested in feelings, behavior, and attitudes. Psychology has many different areas. Some of them are:

- abnormal behavior
- intelligence
- memory
- perception
- child psychology
- social psychology
- sports psychology

The study of psychology began in 1879. William Wundtz started the first psychology research laboratory in that year in Leipzig, Germany.

SOME FAMOUS PSYCHOLOGISTS

Some famous psychologists include:

Ivan Pavlov—Russian, 1849–1936
Sigmund Freud—Austrian, 1856–1939
Alfred Binet—French, 1857–1911
Alfred Adler—Austrian, 1870–1937
Karen Horney—German-American, 1885–1952
C.G. Jung—Swiss, 1875–1961
Carl Rogers—American, 1902–1987
B.F. Skinner—American, 1904–1990

Psychology and You

Psychology is helpful in careers such as nursing, sales, advertising, banking, social work, and management.

Do you want to study psychology? Ask yourself these questions:

- Do I like watching people?
- Am I curious about how people learn?
- Am I interested in human emotions?
- Do I want to learn about memory and how the mind works?

Friendship

CHAPTER PREVIEW

In this chapter, you'll:

Content
▶ read emails between friends
▶ discover the benefits of friendship

Reading Skills
▶ preview a reading by connecting with the topic
▶ identify main ideas in readings

Vocabulary Skills
▶ use words and expressions to describe friends and friendship
▶ use comparison expressions

Writing Skills
▶ write about friends, friendship, and activities with friends

Research Skills
▶ use keywords to do Internet searches
▶ interview people about their friends

SHORT SURVEY

My favorite activity to do with a friend is:

☐ going to the movies

☐ talking

☐ playing sports

☐ studying

☐ other _____

Reading 1:

What do friends say to each other in emails? Read other people's emails and find out.

Reading 2:

Can having just one friend improve your health? Read about some scientific studies on friendship.

What do you think?

What do you like to do with friends on the weekend? Look at the list of activities. Check (✓) your choices. Then ask a partner. Write a check (✓) for your partner's choices.

Weekend Activities	My Friends and I	My Partner & His/Her Friends
Play computer games	_____	_____
See movies	_____	_____
Go shopping	_____	_____
Surf the Internet	_____	_____
Watch TV	_____	_____
Rent a DVD	_____	_____
Go hiking	_____	_____
Go swimming	_____	_____
Go for a bike ride	_____	_____
Play soccer	_____	_____
Play basketball	_____	_____
Make dinner together	_____	_____
Go out for pizza	_____	_____
Have coffee or tea at a café	_____	_____
Play chess	_____	_____
Play ping-pong	_____	_____
Play badminton	_____	_____
Relax and do nothing	_____	_____

Reading 1: Can You Do Me a Favor?

Before You Read

Preview

A. Reading 1 is an email exchange. The title of this reading is "Can You Do Me a Favor?" What do you think it's about? Discuss with a partner.

B. How do you communicate with friends? Complete the following sentences. You can fill in more than one bubble for each sentence.

1. I usually communicate with my friends _____.

   Ⓐ in person   Ⓑ by email   Ⓒ by phone   Ⓓ by instant message (IM)

2. I want to get together with a friend, so I _____.

   Ⓐ call   Ⓑ send an email   Ⓒ send an IM   Ⓓ talk to him or her in person

3. I want to ask a friend for help, so I _____.

   Ⓐ call   Ⓑ send an email   Ⓒ send an IM   Ⓓ talk to him or her in person

4. I want to talk to a friend about a problem, so I _____.

   Ⓐ call

   Ⓑ send an email

   Ⓒ send an IM

   Ⓓ talk to him or her in person

C. Now compare your answers with a partner.

Vocabulary

A. Here are some useful expressions. You can use them to talk about friendship and being a friend. Complete each sentence with the correct expression.

come over	do a favor for	help each other	~~live near each other~~
pay (me) back	pick (it) up	see each other	send emails to each other

1. My best friend goes to school in New York, and I live in San Francisco. I'm sad because we

   don't ____*live*____ ____*near*____ ____*each*____ ____*other*____ .

2. Because my friend lives in New York, we don't _____ _____ _____ very much.

3. My best friend finally got a new computer. Now we can _____ _____

   _____ _____ _____ .

4. Friends _____ _____ _____. For example, my friend gives me a ride to school every day.

5. Sara borrowed five dollars yesterday. She'll _____ _____ _____ tomorrow.

6. There's a good movie on TV Friday night. Do you want to _____ _____ to my house and watch it with me?

7. Can you _____ _____ _____ _____ me? I need a ride to school.

8. Thanks for getting my book for me. I'll come to your apartment and _____

   _____ _____ tomorrow.

B. Descriptive adjectives help us talk about people and things. Here are some words that describe friends and friendship. Work with a partner. Look at each word. Does it describe a friend, a friendship, or both? Write *F* for (Friend), *FS* for (Friendship), and *B* for (Both). The first one is done for you.

____*B*____ close   _____ comfortable   _____ distant   _____ generous

_____ healthy   _____ helpful   _____ relaxed   _____ stressful

As You Read

As you read, think about this question:

▶ What are some words that describe Linda
and Rafael's friendship?

🎧 Can You Do Me a Favor?

Linda and Rafael are friends. They met in first grade. They lived near
each other, and they went to the same schools for 15 years. Now they go to
the same college. They're still good friends. They talk a lot, and they help
each other. They see each other two or three times a week and send emails
5   to each other almost every day.

Here are some of their emails.

From: Rafael Vasquez <rvasquez@rccc.edu>
Date: Wednesday, February 2, 2008 9:05 pm
To: Linda Yee <lyee@rccc.edu>
10   **Subject: Can You Do Me a Favor?**

Hi Linda,

#1   **Can you do a favor for me? I am very busy this week—I don't have time to go to
the bookstore. Can you get the Chemistry 102 book for me? I'm coming over this
weekend, so I can pick it up then.**

15   **By the way, how do you like our chemistry professor? I like her a lot. She
reminds me of our third grade teacher! Do you remember Ms. Kline? ☺**

Rafael

From: Linda Yee <lyee@rccc.edu>
Date: Wednesday, February 2, 2008 10:03 pm
20   **To: Rafael Vasquez <rvasquez@rccc.edu>**
Subject: Re: Can You Do Me a Favor?

Hey Rafael,

#2   **Sure, no problem. I'll get our books. (Can you pay me back this weekend?)**

**I *do* remember Ms. Kline! She was funny. But I'm nervous about chemistry.
25   Chem. 102 is going to be interesting, but it looks a lot harder than Chem. 101.
What do you think?**

See you this weekend.

Linda

From: Rafael Vasquez <rvasquez@rccc.edu>
Date: Monday, February 7, 2008 9:00 pm
To: Linda Yee <lyee@rccc.edu>
Subject: Can I Borrow Your Notes?

Hi Linda,

Chem. 102 is definitely more difficult than Chem. 101. In fact, I didn't
understand everything on Friday. Can I borrow your notes? Your notes are
always neat—they're a lot better than mine!

Rafael

#3

From: Linda Yee <lyee@rccc.edu>
Date: Monday, February 7, 2008 10:32 pm
To: Rafael Vasquez <rvasquez@rccc.edu>
Subject: Re: Can I Borrow Your Notes?

Hi Rafael,

No problem! Of course you can borrow my notes. Let's meet at the café
tomorrow. I'll bring my notes. And don't forget this time—you owe me
$56.00 for the book. I really need the money! Can you bring it tomorrow?
Also, we have the quiz on Friday. Do you want to study together?

Linda

#4

Word Count: 378

Timed Reading

Read "Can You Do Me a Favor?" again.
Read at a comfortable speed. Time
yourself. You will read it again later
and time yourself again.

Start time: _____ (9:05)

End time: _____ (9:08)

My reading time: _____ (3 minutes)

Students
usually have to
read a lot. In each
chapter you will be asked
to do four timed readings.
These timed readings
will help you increase
your reading
speed.

After You Read

Comprehension

A. Circle the words that describe Linda and Rafael's friendship.

close   distant   relaxed

comfortable   healthy   stressful

B. Fill in the bubble for each correct answer.

1. What is the purpose of Email #1?

    (A) to complain   (B) to ask a favor   (C) to make a date

2. Ms. Kline is a _____ teacher.

    (A) Chem. 101   (B) Chem. 102   (C) third grade

3. Based on her emails, which word does *not* describe Linda?

    (A) distant   (B) generous   (C) helpful

4. Why is Linda nervous about Chem. 102?

    (A) The teacher seems mean.   (B) The class seems difficult.

    (C) She doesn't have the book.

5. Why might Rafael ask Linda for favors?

    (A) He probably feels comfortable with her.   (B) He probably asks everyone for favors.

    (C) He thinks that Linda is better at everything than he is.

Talk About It

Talk to a partner about asking friends for help. Describe a time when you asked a friend for help. What did you ask? What happened?

Once I asked my friend to loan me some money.

What happened?

Reading 2: The Benefits of Friendship

Before You Read

Reading Skills

Connecting with the Reading

Good readers connect with readings. They think about the topic of a reading passage and connect their own experience to it. This helps them to make predictions about the reading and understand more as they read.

When you know the topic before you read, try to find some personal connection to it. Then ask yourself questions about the topic. What do you know about the topic? When did you first hear about the topic? Did you study it? Did you read about it?

Here's an example:

Topic	Connection (Questions) → Prediction
The History of American Movies	**Connection:** I like old American movies. What were some of the first American movies? When were they made? Who made them? →
	Prediction: This reading might be about the first American movies and the people who made them.

Now try to connect to this topic. List your connections, questions, and predictions.

Topic	My Connection (Questions) → Predictions
▶ The History of Email	_____
	_____
	_____

Practice

Reading 2 is about the benefits of friendship. Work with a partner. Connect with this topic. Ask questions about it. Make predictions about the reading.

Our Connections (Questions): _____

_____

Our Prediction:
This passage might be about _____

Preview

A. The title of Reading 2 is "The Benefits of Friendship." What do you think it's about? Discuss with a partner.

B. Here are some words and expressions from the reading. Use them to complete the sentences below. The first one is done for you.

benefits	Emotional	Material	~~mentally~~	Patients
physically	recovered	Researchers	scientific studies	

1. A person with a healthy mind is _____*mentally*_____ healthy.

2. A person who doesn't get colds or the flu is probably _____ healthy.

3. _____ collect information. They talk to people, do experiments, and study important documents.

4. _____ are sick people. They are seeing a doctor or staying in a hospital.

5. _____ support is a kind of help that a friend can give. Examples are giving advice, spending time with someone, or listening.

6. _____ support is another kind of help that a friend can give. Examples are loaning money or doing favors.

7. Peter was sick, but now he's better. He _____ quickly.

8. Exercise has many _____. One of the good things about exercise is that it can keep you healthy.

9. Dr. Jones does _____ _____ to find out more about friendship.

As you read, think about this question:
▶ What are the benefits of friendship?

🎧 The Benefits of Friendship

What is friendship? What is a friend? The answer depends on you. What do you like? What do you 5 believe is important? Often friends like the same things. For example, friends often enjoy the same sports, the same movies, or the same 10 music. They enjoy these activities together. Often friends believe the same things, too. For example, two friends might both 15 believe that family is very important, or that it is important to do volunteer work or help save the environment. Two friends might also have similar political ideas.

There are many definitions of "friend." But everyone agrees that it is good to 20 have friends. Friends make you happy. And friendship is good for your health.

Friends keep you healthy. They help to keep you mentally and physically healthy. Many scientific studies show this. For example, a Yale University study compared 194 physically ill people. Some had friends and some didn't. In the group of people with two friends, 63 percent were still alive at the end of one 25 year. In the group of people with no friends, only 43 percent were alive at the end of one year. Researchers at the Behavioral Research Center at Duke University Medical Center discovered the same thing. They studied 1,368 patients with heart disease for nine years. Patients with just one good friend recovered sooner.

30 These studies show the health benefits of friendship. In general, people with friends have better physical health, have better mental health, feel less stress, and live longer than people without friends.

35 Why is this true? The main reason is this: With friends, life is easier. It is easier in two ways. First, friends give emotional support. For example, a friend will listen to your problems. A friend will give advice. A friend will help you

40 make a decision. Friends also give material support. For example, they will loan you money, give you a ride to school, or take care of your pet. These kinds of support make people feel less stressed. And less stress makes people healthier, both physically and mentally.

45 You can have many friends or just one good friend. Either way, research proves the benefits. As the saying goes, "There is no doctor like a true friend."

Word Count: 376

Timed Reading

Read "The Benefits of Friendship" again. Read at a comfortable speed. Time your reading.

Start time: _____

End time: _____

My reading time: _____

After You Read

Reading Skills

Identifying the Main Idea

A reading passage is usually about one important topic or idea. This is the *main* idea. All the information in the passage is related to this main idea. You can often find the main idea at the beginning of the reading and sometimes at the end. The rest of the reading often repeats, explains, and supports this main idea and gives specific examples.

Practice

A. What is the main idea of "The Benefits of Friendship"? Fill in the bubble for the correct answer.

(A) Friends keep you mentally healthy.

(B) Friendship is good for your health.

(C) People with many friends are healthier than people with few friends.

B. Look again at "The Benefits of Friendship." Look for three sentences that express the main idea and underline them. Look in the first few paragraphs and in the last paragraph. In the middle paragraphs, look for repetition of the main idea and for explanations of the main idea using examples.

Getting the Details

A. Answer the questions. Fill in the bubble for each correct answer.

1. What did the Yale University study show?

(A) Physically ill people with friends live longer than physically ill people without friends.

(B) Physically ill people often do not have friends.

(C) Physically ill people without friends live longer than physically ill people with friends.

2. What did the Duke University Medical Research Center study show?

    (A) One friend is not enough to keep you healthy.

    (B) People without friends are more likely to get heart disease.

    (C) People who have a serious illness might recover sooner if they have a friend.

3. What conclusions can you make from the studies in the article?

    (A) People with friends are less happy than people without friends.

    (B) People with friends have harder lives than people without friends.

    (C) People with friends are healthier than people without friends.

4. Which statement is true?

    (A) Scientific studies show that life is less stressful when you have friends.

    (B) There is only one definition of a "friend."

    (C) If you have friends, you never get sick.

5. Which is an example of emotional support?

    (A) taking care of a friend's pet

    (B) loaning money

    (C) listening to a friend's problems

B. Read these sentences from "The Benefits of Friendship." For each one decide if it is a main idea sentence. Circle *Yes* or *No*. The first one is done for you.

	Yes	No
1. Friends keep you healthy.	(Yes)	No
2. First, friends give emotional support.	Yes	No
3. Patients with just one good friend recovered sooner.	Yes	No
4. A friend will give advice.	Yes	No
5. These studies show the health benefits of friendship.	Yes	No
6. In the group of people with two friends, 63 percent were still alive at the end of one year.	Yes	No

Vocabulary

A. Here are some more words and expressions from "The Benefits of Friendship." Find them in the reading and circle them.

Noun	Verbs	Expression
political ideas	feel less stress do volunteer work	save the environment

B. Now use the words to fill in the blanks below.

1. My friends and I have similar _____ _____. In fact, we all voted for the same president in the last election.

2. Recycling paper, cans, and bottles can help _____ _____ _____.

3. I _____ _____ _____ now because a friend helps me with my homework.

4. My friend and I pick up trash at the beach in our free time. We don't get paid. We like to

_____ _____ _____.

Talk About It

Discuss the following questions:

1. What is your definition of "friend"?

2. A classmate wants to make new friends. What do you suggest? How do people start new friendships? How do people keep friends?

To me, a friend is someone who...

Really? To me a friend is...

Expressions

Making Comparisons

The passages in this chapter have several comparative expressions such as *is harder than*. We use comparative forms of adjectives to compare two things. Usually, one and two-syllable adjectives add *–er*. Adjectives with three or more syllables use the words *more* and *less*.

Examples: Chem. 102 <u>is harder than</u> Chem. 101.

Chem. 102 <u>is more difficult than</u> Chem. 101.

Sometimes people compare two things without the second item.
Example: Life <u>is easier</u> with friends. (The writer didn't add *than without friends*.)

You can also compare with adverbs.
Example: People with friends <u>live longer</u>.

Practice

A. Find and underline these comparative expressions in "Can You Do Me a Favor?" or "The Benefits of Friendship."

> are better than   makes people healthier than   is more difficult than
> live longer than   recovered sooner than

B. Now use the comparative expressions to complete the following sentences.

1. Some studies show that having a pet _____ _____ _____ _____ not having one.

2. According to some studies, people who have pets _____ _____ _____ people who don't have pets.

3. Linda always gets As. Her grades _____ _____ _____ mine.

4. English _____ _____ _____ _____ Spanish because English spelling is irregular.

5. Both Linda and Rafael got the flu, but Rafael _____ _____ _____ Linda because he stayed in bed.

Internet Research

Using Search Engines and Keywords

A search engine looks for information on the Internet. To do this, it uses *keywords*. Keywords identify the main ideas in webpages. You can combine keywords with the word *and* to get exactly what you want. Little words such as *in* and *the* aren't important. To start a search, go to a search engine like Google (www.google.com). Type your keyword(s) into the text box and then click the "Search" button. Example:

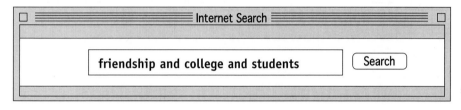

The search engine will show you a list of webpages on the topic.

Practice

Practice using keywords. Work in small groups. List possible keywords for the following searches. You want to find information on:

▶ another scientific study (such as the one from Yale University) on the health benefits of friendship

▶ a place to go hiking with a friend in your area

▶ a quote about friendship

▶ information on the health benefits of pets

▶ your own topic

Now choose one of the above topics. Open a search engine, such as Google. Try the keywords from your list. Tell the class about your search.

▶ Which keywords did you use?

▶ Did you combine keywords?

▶ Did you get the information you wanted?

▶ Why or why not?

Write About It

A. Write the following paragraphs. Fill in the blanks. Write complete sentences.

Paragraph One

Making friends can be easy. One way to meet new friends is _____
[Give one way to meet new friends]

_____. This is a good way because _____
[Explain why it is a good way]

_____. Another way to meet a new friend is _____

_____. This is also a good way because _____
[Give another way to meet new friends]

_____.
[Explain why it is a good way]

Paragraph Two

_____ is not like me. First of all, she/he is _____
[Name of person]

_____. For example, _____
[Use a comparison expression]

_____. Also, she/he is _____
[Give an example]

_____. For example,
[Use another comparison expression]

_____.
[Give an example]

B. Now write your own paragraphs. First, write one paragraph about how to meet new friends. Then write another one that compares you and another person. Try to include three new words or expressions from this chapter in your paragraphs.

C. Write one more paragraph about friends and friendship. Here are some ideas:

▶ Write about a time that you asked a friend for help.

▶ Compare two friends.

▶ Compare two weekend activities you do with your friends.

▶ Explain a quote on friendship.

Include three new words or expressions from this chapter in your paragraphs. Also, try to use your Internet research.

On Your Own

Project

Take a survey. Ask your classmates about their friends.

Step 1: Practice

Listen as your teacher reads the friendship survey questions below. Do you understand them? Repeat them after your teacher so you can pronounce them correctly.

Step 2: Take a Survey

Ask a classmate questions about his/her friends. Use the form below.

Friendship Survey

Name _____

1. Who is your oldest friend?

   _____

2. When did you meet?

   _____

3. How do you communicate with each other (for example, email, IM, telephone)?

   _____

4. How often do you see each other?

   _____

5. What activities to you do together?

   _____

   _____

6. Where are you from?

   _____

Step 3: Follow-Up

Explain the results of your survey to the class.

Wrap Up

How Much Do You Remember?

Check your new knowledge. In this chapter, you learned facts, words, and expressions. You also learned reading skills and you practiced writing. Complete the following to check what you remember.

1. Why is friendship good for your health?

   _____

2. Describe one of your friends. Use a descriptive adjective.

   _____

3. Use *live near each other* in a sentence.

   _____

4. Where can you find the main ideas in a reading passage?

   _____

5. Give an example of emotional support. Give an example of material support.

   _____

   _____

6. Explain an interesting result from your survey.

   _____

Second Timed Readings

Now reread "Can You Do Me a Favor?" and "The Benefits of Friendship." Time each reading separately. Write your times for all Timed Readings in this chapter in the Timed Reading Chart on page 212.

Crossword Puzzle

Complete the crossword puzzle to practice some words and expressions from this chapter.

CLUES

Across →
3. Rafael said, "I'll _____ _____ tomorrow and get my book."
5. If you borrow money, you should _____ it _____ soon.
6. The opposite of "distant"
7. Having to do with feelings
8. The opposite of "relaxed"

Down ↓
1. People with friends are _____ healthy.
2. They collect information for scientific studies.
4. Loaning money is an example of this kind of support.

Finding Lost Loves

CHAPTER PREVIEW

In this chapter, you'll:

Content
▶ read an interview with two young people in love
▶ read a research study about "lost loves"

Reading Skills
▶ use reading titles to make predictions
▶ identify details in a reading

Vocabulary Skills
▶ use words and expressions to talk about love and romance
▶ use words and expressions to talk about research

Writing Skills
▶ write about love and romance

Research Skills
▶ limit search results on the Internet
▶ interview people about their ideal mates

SHORT SURVEY

What is most important to you in a romantic partner?

❑ good looks

❑ intelligence

❑ money

❑ sense of humor

❑ other _____

Reading 1:
What could happen if you met a love from the past? Read about Mia and Jordan to find out.

Reading 2:
Nancy Kalish asked 1,000 people about their lost loves. What did she discover? Read about her study.

What do you think?

Find your ideal romantic partner. First, tell us about YOU. Check (✓) the best answer(s) for you. If the answer is "other," explain. Discuss your answers with a partner.

Romantic Partners, Inc.

1. The ideal first date:

   ____ coffee in a café   ____ a walk on the beach   ____ a movie   ____ other _____

2. Your favorite hangout:

   ____ a café   ____ a bar   ____ a restaurant   ____ a bookstore   ____ other _____

3. Money is _____ important.

   ____ extremely   ____ very   ____ not so   ____ not at all

4. My favorite food:

   ____ Mexican   ____ Italian   ____ Japanese   ____ Chinese   ____ other _____

5. My favorite music:

   ____ rock   ____ classical   ____ hip-hop   ____ other _____

6. My favorite physical activities:

   ____ walking   ____ biking   ____ playing basketball   ____ yoga   ____ other _____

7. These pets are O.K. with me:

   ____ dog   ____ cat   ____ bird   ____ fish   ____ none   ____ other _____

8. My personality traits:

   ____ quiet   ____ shy   ____ loving   ____ funny   ____ other _____

Now answer this question: Is your ideal partner someone similar to you or different from you?

_____

Reading 1: Lost Loves: One Couple's Story

Before You Read

Preview

A. The title of Reading 1 is "Lost Loves: One Couple's Story." What do you think it's about? Discuss with a partner.

B. Take the following quiz. Fill in the bubble for each correct answer.

1. At what age do people usually start elementary school in the United States?

(A) 3 or 4   (B) 5 or 6

(C) 13 or 14   (D) 17 or 18

2. At what age do people usually start high school in the United States?

(A) 3 or 4   (B) 5 or 6

(C) 13 or 14   (D) 17 or 18

3. At what age do people usually graduate from high school in the United States?

(A) 13 or 14   (B) 15 or 16

(C) 17 or 18   (D) 21 or 22

4. At what age do people usually graduate from college in the United States?

(A) 18   (B) 22

(C) 20   (D) 24

5. At what age do people usually get married in the United States?

(A) 20   (B) 30

(C) 25   (D) It depends.

Vocabulary

A. Here are some expressions used to describe feelings of love. Some are for stronger feelings, some are for weaker feelings, and some are in between. Put each word or phrase in the correct column. One is done for you.

adore	be crazy about	be fond of	be in love with	~~be mad about~~
care for	like	love	worship	

Stronger	In Between	Weaker
be mad about		

B. Here are some more expressions used to discuss romance and relationships. Match the expressions with their meanings. Write the letter of each meaning next to the correct expression. The first one is done for you.

_f_ **1.** break up   **a.** start being in love

____ **2.** fall in love   **b.** someone who is perfect for you

____ **3.** get married   **c.** move away from

____ **4.** lost love   **d.** become husband and wife

____ **5.** partner   **e.** the other person in a couple

____ **6.** separate   **f.** end a relationship

____ **7.** soul mate   **g.** someone whom you loved in the past, and still love, but do not see

As you read, think about these questions:

▶ Did Mia and Jordan always love each other? How do you know?

At one glance
I love you
With a thousand hearts. 🐦

—*Mihri Hatun (Turkish poet, died 1506)*

🎧 Lost Loves: One Couple's Story

Mia and Jordan met a long time ago. They met when they were children. At that time, they were best friends and were always together. Then Jordan's family moved away. Mia
and Jordan couldn't see each other. But they met again, many years later. When
5   they met, something special happened.

Rosa Gutierrez, a reporter, was interested in their story, so she interviewed them on her TV show.

Here is her interview:

Rosa Gutierrez: Today, we are going to meet Mia and Jordan. Mia and Jordan
10 are lost loves. Mia, when did you and Jordan first meet?

Mia: Jordan and I went to the same elementary school.

Jordan: Yeah. In fact, Mia was my best friend. I always wanted to be with her.

Rosa Gutierrez: So what happened? When did you separate?

Jordan: When I was 15 years old, my family moved away.

15 **Rosa Gutierrez:** How did you feel?

Jordan: Very sad. I thought, "We're soul mates." Mia and I belong together. I felt so sad.
I never forgot about Mia.

Rosa Gutierrez: Then what happened?

20 **Mia:** We grew up and went to college. We had new boyfriends and girlfriends.

Jordan: Yeah. We were busy. We never saw each other. We wrote for a couple of years and then we stopped. But we never forgot each other.

Rosa Gutierrez: When did you meet again?

Mia: I graduated from college last May. I went to a big graduation party that a friend was having. Jordan was there. We were very surprised to see each other. I had no idea that my friend was also friends with Jordan.

Rosa Gutierrez: And what happened?

Jordan: We were very happy to see each other. We went to dinner the next night.

Mia: We talked a lot. We had a lot in common.

Jordan: And we started dating.

Mia: And we fell in love!

Jordan: Yeah, we've been dating for about one year. We're together all the time now. I'm so happy to be with Mia again.

Rosa Gutierrez: What happens next?

Mia/Jordan: We're going to get married next year!

Word Count: 349

Timed Reading

Read "Lost Loves: One Couple's Story" again. Read at a comfortable speed. Time your reading.

Start time: _____

End time: _____

My reading time: _____

After You Read

Comprehension

A. Did Mia and Jordan always love each other? How do you know? Write your answer on the line.

_____

B. Fill in the bubble for each correct answer.

1. Jordan and Mia were together _____.

   Ⓐ during elementary school   Ⓑ for part of high school

   Ⓒ both A and B

2. Jordan and Mia met again _____.

   Ⓐ before college   Ⓑ during college   Ⓒ after college

3. They met again _____.

   Ⓐ at a wedding party   Ⓑ at a birthday party   Ⓒ at a graduation party

4. The party was for _____.

   Ⓐ a friend of Mia's   Ⓑ a friend of Jordan's   Ⓒ a friend of Mia and Jordan's

5. What are Mia and Jordan's plans?

   Ⓐ They are going to dinner.   Ⓑ They are going to order dessert.

   Ⓒ They are going to get married.

Talk About It

Discuss soul mates. Ask and answer the following questions:

1. Do you believe in soul mates? Why or why not?

2. Is there one special person for everyone?

Reading 2: The Lost Love Study

Before You Read

Reading Skills

Using the Title to Predict

In Chapter 1, you used the topic of the reading to make predictions. You can also learn more about the main idea of the reading from the title. Plus, you can *go beyond* (think of more ideas about) the main idea and guess more about the reading. This helps you prepare for the reading. It makes the reading easier to understand. Here is the title of a reading in this book and a sample prediction:

Title	Prediction
"Food Names in the United States" (page 55)	This reading is about the names of foods in the United States. **Go beyond →** It might also be about where food names come from or about different food names in different parts of the country.

Here are some reading titles from this book. Make predictions of what each is about.

Titles	Predictions
▶ "Athletes and the Laws of Physics" (page 97)	_____ _____
▶ "Sports and History " (page 117)	_____ _____
▶ "Twins: Separated at Birth" (page 134)	_____ _____

Practice

The title of Reading 2 is "The Lost Love Study." What do you think it's about? Go beyond your first prediction to make two more predictions about the reading. Discuss your predictions with a partner.

Predictions: _____

Preview

Here are some words and expressions from Reading 2. Use them to complete the sentences below.

> human emotions   included   interested in
> participant   reconnected   renewed their relationship

1. The professor was _____ _____ lost loves, so she decided to do a study.

2. Josh was a part of the professor's study. He enjoyed being a _____.

3. The professor studied both old and young people. She _____ all ages in her study.

4. The psychologist studied people's feelings. She was particularly interested in love, the

strongest of all the _____ _____.

5. Mia met her lost love later on in life. She was very happy when she

_____ with him.

6. Jim and Sue were friends in the past. Then they were separated. They met again at college and

_____ _____

_____.

As you read, think about this question:

► Are lost-love relationships stronger or
   weaker than other relationships?

> **All our loves are
> first loves.** 🐌
>
> —*Susan Fromberg Schaeffer
> (American author, b. 1966)*

🎧 The Lost Love Study

Sociologists and psychologists study human emotions, such
as love and romance. Sociologists are usually interested in
emotions and social groups. Psychologists are usually
interested in emotions and individuals. Studies of human
5   emotion help us to understand ourselves and the people
around us better.

One psychologist, Dr. Nancy Kalish of California State
University, was interested in a kind of love called "lost love."
She wondered about lost loves. She knew lost loves were
10   people who were in love, separated, and met again later in
life. Sometimes they met after 20 years, and sometimes after
30 years. Sometimes they even met 50 years later. Dr. Kalish
wondered what happened after they reunited.

Dr. Kalish conducted a study. She collected information from over 1,000
15   people. Each person had a "lost love." Each person renewed their relationship
with their lost love. Dr. Kalish asked these people to talk about their "lost love."
She asked them many questions: When did you first meet? How long were you
together? Why did you separate? How did you find your lost love?

Dr. Kalish received information from all 50 U.S. states and from 33 countries.
20   These countries included Egypt, India, Russia, and Thailand. Two-thirds of the
people were female. One-third was male. The youngest participant was 18. The
oldest was 89. One couple met in high school. They reconnected 63 years later,
and they married at age 80!

What Happens to "Lost Loves"?

Dr. Kalish learned several interesting facts about the lost loves in her study:

25
- 84 percent fell in love before they were 22 years old.
- 50 percent renewed their romance in their late 20s to 30s.
- 33 percent renewed their romance at ages 40 to 50.
- 25 percent lived within 50 miles of each other.
- 36 percent lived farther than 1,000 miles.

30 In general, Dr. Kalish learned this about lost love relationships: They are very strong. They often result in marriage, and lost love marriages last longer than other marriages. In fact, 50 percent of marriages in the United States end in divorce. Seventy-five percent of lost loves stay together.

Why is this true? From her study, Dr. Kalish came to a conclusion. Many 35 young people have strong feelings. For many young people, the first love relationship is very important. These important feelings usually don't go away, and if the couple does meet again, the strong feelings can come back.

Word Count: 398

Timed Reading

Read "The Lost Love Study" again. Read at a comfortable speed. Time your reading.

Start time: _____

End time: _____

My reading time: _____

After You Read

Main Idea

What was the main thing Dr. Kalish learned from her study? Fill in the bubble for the correct answer.

(A) Lost love relationships end in divorce 50 percent of the time.

(B) Lost love relationships are stronger than other relationships.

(C) Thirty-six percent of lost loves lived farther than 1,000 miles from each other.

Reading Skills

Looking for Details

When you read, it's important to get the general or main ideas. It is also important to find and understand the details. Details often answer a reader's questions about the main ideas. Details also support and explain main ideas. They are usually facts, examples, or explanations. When you look for details, look for numbers, lists, and sentences that explain words and ideas.

Examples:

Dr. Kalish conducted a study. (Reader's Question: How did she conduct it?) → She collected information from over 1,000 people. (This sentence explains how.)

Dr. Kalish received information from ... 33 countries. (Reader's Question: Which countries?) → These countries included Egypt, India, Russia, and Thailand. (This sentence gives some examples.)

Practice

A. Find details in the reading to answer these questions. Look for numbers, lists, and sentences that explain words and ideas.

1. How many people sent Dr. Kalish questionnaires? _____

2. What are "lost loves"? _____

3. What percentage of the participants were male? _____

4. How old was the youngest participant? _____

5. What percentage of lost loves stay together after they are married? _____

B. With a partner, complete the chart. Find a detail in the article for each quantity (numerals and written numbers). The first one is done for you.

Quantity	Details
1,000	*number of people in Kalish's study*
two-thirds	
50	
63	
36 percent	

Vocabulary

A. Here are some expressions from "The Lost Love Study." Find them in the reading and circle them.

> come back   end in   go away
> result in   talked about   wondered about

B. Now use them to complete the sentences below. Sometimes more than one item can be correct.

1. "I didn't know if she loved me. I kept asking myself. I always _____ _____ it, but we never talked about it," Michael said.

2. When lost loves find each other, they often fall in love again. The new relationships often

   _____ _____ marriage.

3. The new relationships also seldom _____ _____ divorce.

4. Mia always loved Jordan. Her feelings didn't _____ _____.

5. Strong feelings don't often disappear. They often _____ _____ many years later.

6. She loved to talk, and when she talked, she always _____ _____ Jordan.

Talk About It

Discuss the following questions:

1. Your friend wants to find a boyfriend/girlfriend. What's a good way to meet someone?

2. Do you know someone with a "lost love" experience? If so, share the story with the group.

What's a good way to meet someone?

You can...

Expressions

Doing Research

We use certain words and expressions to describe research, interviews, and studies. Many are combinations of verbs and nouns. For example, look at this sentence:

Dr. Kalish <u>conducted a study</u>.
Verb + Noun

Practice

A. Find and underline these research expressions in "Lost Loves: One Couple's Story" or "The Lost Love Study."

collected information	came to a conclusion	learned (something) about
conducted a study	is/was interested in	received information

B. Now use the research expressions to complete the following sentences.

1. Rosa _____ _____

   _____ human behavior, so she studies psychology in college.

2. Rosa wanted find out how people study for exams, so she _____

   _____ _____. She asked several people the same question.

3. Rosa _____ _____ from 100 people. She got answers from everyone.

4. Rosa also sent emails to people. This way, she _____

   _____ _____ people in other countries.

5. Rosa _____ _____

   _____ students: many stay up late the night before an exam.

6. Rosa _____ _____

   _____ _____: Students do better on exams when they don't stay up late.

Internet Research

Limiting a Search

When you do a search on the Internet, sometimes you get *too much* information. For example, if you search for *romance* you can get over 35,000,000 results! *Romance* is a very general term. If you search for *Nancy Kalish,* you can get over 6,000 results. In Chapter 1, you combined keywords. For example, if you do a combined keyword search for *Nancy Kalish* and *lost and found loves,* you get fewer results. To limit a search even more, use quotation marks [" "] around key phrases. For example, if you search for *"Nancy Kalish lost and found loves,"* you will get only a few results because your keywords are specific and they are in quotations.

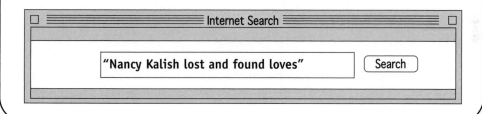

Practice

Practice using quotations to limit a search. First, use keywords without quotations. Then use keywords with quotations. What is the difference? Try looking for the following:

▶ lost love

▶ an old romantic partner's name (Example: Lance Beard)

▶ your first name, your last name, your first and last name

▶ one of your friend's names

▶ your choice

Tell the class about your experience.

Write About It

A. Write the following paragraphs. Fill in the blanks. Write complete sentences.

Paragraph One

The best thing to do on a first date is _____ .
                                                        [Give an activity]

This is good because _____
                                          [Explain the reason]

_____ . The worst thing to do on a first date is _____ .
                                                                    [Give an activity]

_____ . This is not a good first date because _____
                                                                  [Explain the reason]

_____ .

Paragraph Two

I am looking for two important things in a mate: _____ and
                                                  [Write an important thing]

_____ . _____ is important because _____
   [Write an important thing]   [Write the first thing]   [Explain the reason]

_____ . _____ is important because
                              [Write the second thing]

_____ .
                              [Explain the reason]

B. Now write your own paragraphs. First, write a paragraph about good and bad first dates. Then write another one about your ideal mate.

C. Write more paragraphs about love and romance. Here are some ideas:

▶ Describe your first love.

▶ Write about the best way to find a romantic partner.

▶ Answer this question: Can past loves be friends? Why or why not?

▶ Write about the best age to start dating.

▶ Your own idea

Include three new words or expressions from this chapter in your paragraphs. Also, try to use your Internet research.

On Your Own

Project

Take a survey. Ask your classmates about their ideal mates.

Step 1: Practice

Listen as your teacher reads the Ideal Mate Survey questions below. Do you understand them? Repeat them after your teacher so you can pronounce them correctly.

Step 2: Take a Survey

Ask five classmates questions about their ideal romantic partners. Indicate *M* (male) or *F* (female) for each person. Use one copy of the form for each classmate.

Ideal Mate Survey

Name _____   M _____   F _____

1. Is your ideal romantic partner older than you, younger than you, or the same age as you?

   _____

2. Does your ideal mate earn more money than you, less money than you, or the same amount of money as you?

   _____

3. What are your ideal mate's hobbies?

   _____

4. Does your ideal mate like to sleep late or get up early in the morning?

   _____

5. What is the most important thing about your ideal mate?

   _____

6. Where are you from?

   _____

Step 3: Follow-Up

Explain the results of your survey to the class.

Wrap Up

How Much Do You Remember?

Check your new knowledge. In this chapter, you learned facts, words, and expressions. You also learned reading skills and you practiced writing. Complete the following to check what you remember.

1. Give one fact about lost loves.

   _____

   _____

2. Use one of the research expressions on page 38 to describe Nancy Kalish's study.

   _____

   _____

3. Which love expression is stronger, *be crazy about* or *be fond of*?

   _____

4. Use *come back* in a sentence.

   _____

5. How can you find details in a reading?

   _____

6. What is one way to limit an Internet search?

   _____

Second Timed Readings

Now reread "Lost Loves: One Couple's Story" and "The Lost Love Study." Time each reading separately. Write your times for all the Timed Readings in this chapter in the Timed Reading Chart on page 212.

Crossword Puzzle

Complete the crossword puzzle to practice some words from this chapter.

CLUES

Across →

3. End a relationship

6. Mia and Jordan separated, then met again and _____ their relationship.

7. Mia and Jordan are _____.

8. Someone who takes part in a study

Down ↓

1. Husband, wife, mate, boyfriend, or girlfriend

2. Love, joy, hate, and sadness are all examples of this.

4. Love strongly

5. Someone who is perfect for you

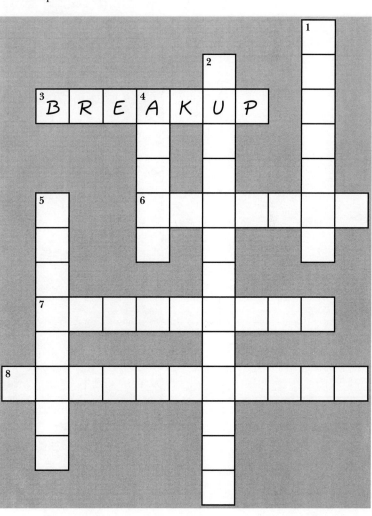

What is Nutrition?

Nutrition is the study of food and health. Nutritionists study the biological, biochemical, physiological, sociological, and psychological aspects of food. Some of the areas that nutritionists are interested in include:

- diets (for example, for young people, for old people, in different cultures)
- food safety
- food service management
- health and nutrition in developing nations
- consumer protection

People have always been interested in food and health. The study of nutrition began thousands of years ago. For example, in 400 B.C., Hippocrates, the "Father of Medicine," said to his students, "Let thy food be thy medicine and thy medicine be thy food."

SOME FAMOUS NUTRITIONISTS

Some of the scientists who made important discoveries about nutrition include:

James Lind—British naval physician, 1716–1794. Discovered that Vitamin C prevents scurvy.

Antoine Lavoisier—French chemist, 1743–1794. Discovered how food is metabolized.

Christiaan Eijkman—Dutch physician, 1858–1930. Discovered that Vitamin B1 can cure beriberi.

Sir Frederick Gowland Hopkins—British biochemist, 1861–1947. Won the Nobel prize for his work with vitamins.

Casimir Funk—Polish biochemist, 1884–1967. The first person to use the word "vitamin."

Linus Pauling—American chemist, 1901–1994. Researched the role of vitamins in maintaining physical and mental health.

Nutrition and You

People who study nutrition work in health care, government, international agencies, food service, research, food manufacturing, culinary training, and the media.

Do you want to study nutrition? Ask yourself these questions:

- Do I like to help people?
- Am I interested in improving health?
- Do I wonder about what is in food?
- Am I interested in what and why people eat?
- Do I like science, particularly biology and chemistry?

CHAPTER **3** # Food Names

> **A smiling face is
> half the meal.** 🍃
>
> —*Latvian proverb*

CHAPTER PREVIEW

In this chapter, you'll:

Content
▶ read a true story about a restaurant server and a customer
▶ learn food names in the United States

Reading Skills
▶ preview by using titles and headings
▶ identify examples in a reading

Vocabulary Skills
▶ use words and expressions to talk about food
▶ use expressions with verbs + prepositions

Writing Skills
▶ write about food

Research Skills
▶ use an online food dictionary
▶ interview people about food and eating

SHORT SURVEY

What's your favorite lunchtime food?
- ❏ pizza
- ❏ hamburger
- ❏ noodles
- ❏ salad
- ❏ other _____

Reading 1:

Do all Americans speak the same language? Not always! Read about a misunderstanding in a restaurant.

Reading 2:

Do buffalo wings come from buffaloes? Read about some unusual food names in English.

What do you think?

What kind of food do you like? Use the menu below and check (✓) your choices. Then ask a partner: "What would you like?" Write a check (✓) for your partner's choices.

Pine Valley Café

"Comfort food . . . like Mom used to make."

Today's Menu

Soups & Salads	My Partner	Me
Chef salad	_____	_____
Three-bean salad	_____	_____
Baby greens (choice of dressing)	_____	_____
Tomato soup	_____	_____
Onion soup	_____	_____
Soup du jour	_____	_____

Main Courses

Pizza (cheese, sausage, or vegetable)	_____	_____
Lasagna	_____	_____
Chili con carne	_____	_____
Grilled salmon (with baked potato and baby vegetables)	_____	_____
Hangar steak (with garlic mashed potatoes and baby vegetables)	_____	_____

Desserts

Cheesecake	_____	_____
Brownie with ice cream	_____	_____
Apple pie	_____	_____

Pine Valley Café

21 E. 18th Street
New York, NY 10014
212-555-4586

Chef: Maria Salazar   Visit us on the Web! www.pinevalleycafe.com

Reading 1: Soup du Jour

Before You Read

Preview

A. The title of Reading 1 is *"Soup du Jour."* What do you think it's about? Discuss with a partner.

B. Take the quiz. Fill in the bubble for each correct answer.

1. What does *soup du jour* mean?

    (A) Soup made with tomatoes.

    (B) Soup made with noodles.

    (C) Soup "of the day" or today's special soup.

2. What language is *soup du jour*?

    (A) Italian

    (B) French

    (C) English

Vocabulary

A. English has many foreign words. Here are some foreign food names that we use in English. Match each food name with the correct language. Write the letter of the language next to the food. The first one is done for you.

   c pizza   **a.** French

   _____ croissant   **b.** Spanish

   _____ burrito   ~~c.~~ Italian

   _____ dim sum   **d.** Chinese

   _____ sushi   **e.** Thai

   _____ pad thai   **f.** Japanese

B. Now discuss these questions in small groups: What are the foods listed in Activity A? Which of these foods have you eaten? How did you like them?

C. In small groups, write the name of the countries on the map.

| China | France | Italy |
| Japan | Spain | Thailand |

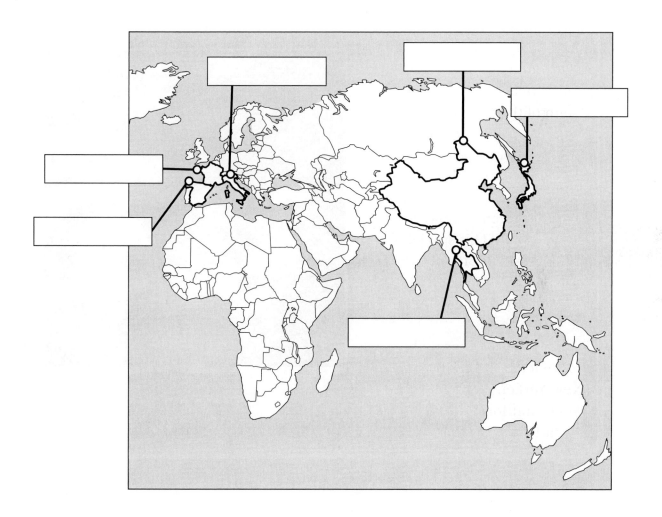

As You Read

As you read, think about these questions:

▶ What problem did David Rifkin have? How did he solve it?

🎧 *Soup du Jour*

Sometimes even people who speak the same language have trouble communicating. The following conversation is an example. It's a misunderstanding between a server and a customer. The customer

5   knows that *soup du jour* means "soup of the day." (*Soup du jour* is French. Many restaurants in the U.S. have a *soup du jour*. Most English speakers know

10   what it means) This means that the restaurant has a special soup. This special soup changes every day. One day it may be chicken soup, for

15   example. The next day it may be pea soup.

    This is a true story. The customer, David Rifkin, is a New Yorker. He went to a local restaurant for dinner. He asked about the *soup du jour*.

Here is his conversation with the server:

David: What kind of soup do you have tonight?

20 **Server:** We have *soup du jour.*

David: Yes, I know. What kind of soup is it?

Server: It's *soup du jour.*

David: You don't understand. What type of soup do you have?

Server: It's *soup du jour.*

25 **David:** Forget about it. Bring me a hamburger, please.

Adapted from Metropolitan Diary, *New York Times*

Word Count: 182

Timed Reading

Read *"Soup du Jour"* again. Read at a comfortable speed. Time your reading.

Start time: _____

End time: _____

My reading time: _____

After You Read

Comprehension

Fill in the bubble for each correct answer.

1. What does David Rifkin want to order?

   (A) salad   (B) soup   (C) *dim sum*

2. What does *soup du jour* mean to David?

   (A) soup of the day   (B) tomato soup   (C) noodle soup

3. What does *soup du jour* mean to the server?

   (A) She thinks it's the soup of the day.

   (B) She thinks it's the name of a kind of soup.

   (C) She doesn't know what it means.

4. What is the problem?

   (A) The server doesn't know what *soup du jour* means.

   (B) David knows what *soup du jour* means.

   (C) both A and B

5. How does David solve the problem?

   (A) He orders a hamburger.

   (B) He gets mad.

   (C) He leaves the restaurant.

Talk About It

Tell a partner about a problem that you had at a restaurant.

What problem did you have?

I went to a café. I wanted . . . but I didn't get that. I got . . .

Reading 2: The Language of Food

Before You Read

Reading Skills

Using Titles and Headings to Make Predictions

In Chapter 2, you learned about using titles to make predictions about the reading passage. Good readers also use headings to make predictions. Headings usually tell you what a section of the reading is about. Titles and headings are usually in large or bold type. Example:

Regions of the United States (Title)

Part One: New England (Heading)
New England is on the east coast of the United States. Six states make up New England; they are Connecticut, Maine, Massachusetts, New Hampshire, Rhode Island, and Vermont.

Part Two: The Midwest (Another Heading)
The Midwest is in the central part of the United States. Eight states make up the Midwest; they are Illinois, Indiana, Iowa, Ohio, Michigan, Minnesota, Missouri, and Wisconsin.

Practice

Practice using titles and headings to make predictions. Look at "The Language of Food " on pages 55–56 and answer the following questions. Fill in the bubble for each correct answer.

1. Look at the title of the reading. Which of these topics do you think it is about?

   Ⓐ food names   Ⓑ strange food names   Ⓒ English food names

2. Read the first heading. What do you think this section is about?

   Ⓐ English food names   Ⓑ strange food names

   Ⓒ food names from other countries

3. Read the second heading. What do you think this section is about?

   Ⓐ foreign food names   Ⓑ English food names

   Ⓒ food names don't describe the food.

4. Read the third heading. What do you think this section is about?

   Ⓐ Different parts of the world use different food names.

   Ⓑ There are a lot of food names in the United States.

   Ⓒ No matter where you are in the United States, people use the same food words.

Preview

A. The title of Reading 2 is "The Language of Food." What do you think it's about? Discuss with a partner.

B. Here are some food words from the reading. Match each food with the correct picture. Write the letter of the picture next to the food.

a.   b.   c.   d.

_____ buffalo wings   _____ eggplant   _____ seltzer   _____ submarine sandwich

As you read, think about this question:
▶ Where do food names come from?

🎧 The Language of Food

Foreign Food Names

English has many foreign words. Many of these words are food names. How do foreign food words come into English? Some food words come with immigrants. Immigrants come to English-speaking countries. They bring their favorite foods from their countries, and they also bring the names. These foods often become
5   popular. English speakers like the foods and use the original "foreign" names. Sometimes there is an English word for the same thing, but people like the original name for the food. For example, the Italian word *pasta* means about the same thing as the English word *noodles*, but English speakers often use the Italian word.

Travel is another way foreign food words become a part of a language. For
10 example, many English speakers travel in Europe. They enjoy food and drink such as *croissants* (crescent rolls) and *lattes* (coffee with milk). They want to enjoy the same food and drink at home, so restaurants and cafés serve them. Today, in almost every café, you see *croissants* and *lattes* on the menu. Here are some more examples of foreign food words that are found on many American menus: *salsa* (Spanish for
15 "sauce"), *chai* (the East Indian word for "tea"), *sauerkraut* (German for "sour cabbage"), and *tofu* (Chinese for "bean curd").

Food Names Hide Meanings

Food names sometimes hide the true identity of a food. For example, American cowboys had to eat beans, beans, and more
20 beans. Because of this, they made up new names for the beans to make themselves laugh. They renamed beans "Arizona strawberries." This is funny because cowboys usually worked in dry places, such as
25 Arizona. Strawberries don't grow in dry places, so cowboys never ate them.

At one time in New York City, a popular drink was the egg cream. This drink had no egg in it. It had no cream in it. An egg cream was milk mixed with chocolate syrup and seltzer water. At that time, eggs were expensive. People felt like they were ordering an expensive food when they said the name.

And what about buffalo wings? Here's another food that doesn't match its name. First of all, buffaloes don't have wings. Buffalo wings are actually chicken wings. Teressa Bellissimo, a cook from the city of Buffalo in New York, invented the name one day when she had cooked too many chicken wings.

One Food, Many Names

Food words also differ from country to country. This happens even when two countries have the same language. Take the United States and England for example. A cookie in the United States is a biscuit in England; a shrimp in the United States is a prawn in England; and an eggplant in the United States is an aubergine in England.

Also, within the same country, food words aren't always the same. Food names can change depending on the region you are in. For instance, if you want a soft drink in New England, ask for a soda. This works in most parts of the United States, except in the Midwest. Look at a menu in the Midwest—there, a soft drink is called a pop.

There are even more names for big sandwiches. They're called submarines in many parts of the country. They're called hoagies in Pennsylvania, grinders in New England, and po'boys ("poor boys") in New Orleans.

Food names in English can come from foreign words. They don't always tell you exactly what the food is, and they differ from region to region. Everyone cares about food. Maybe that's why most languages have a lot of words for talking about it.

Word Count: 599

Timed Reading

Read the "The Language of Food" again. Read at a comfortable speed. Time your reading.

Start time: _____

End time: _____

My reading time: _____

After You Read

Main Idea

What is the main idea of "The Language of Food"? Fill in the bubble for the correct answer.

Some food names in the United States _____.

- (A) come from foreign words
- (B) change from place to place
- (C) sometimes hide their true meanings
- (D) all of the above
- (E) none of the above

Getting the Details

A. Fill in the bubble for each correct answer.

1. What is one reason there are foreign food names in English?

    - (A) because English has many foreign words
    - (B) because immigrants and travelers bring foreign food names to English speakers
    - (C) because there is no English word for some foods

2. The food name *buffalo wings* is an example of _____.

    - (A) a food that came from buffaloes
    - (B) a food that cowboys ate
    - (C) a food name that doesn't tell you what it is

3. Which statement is NOT true?

    - (A) A *cookie* in the U.S. is a *biscuit* in England.
    - (B) Sometimes one food has more than one name.
    - (C) Big sandwiches are always called *hoagies* in the United States.

Reading Skills

Finding Examples

Good writers give you examples. Examples help you understand the writer's ideas. Examples help explain ideas. They help the writer explain or prove ideas. Underlined below are some expressions that introduce examples:

► Food names differ within the United States. <u>For example</u>, in New England people call a soft drink a "soda," but it's called a "pop" in the Midwest.

► There are even more names for big sandwiches. <u>For instance</u>, they're called *submarines* in many parts of the country.

► They enjoy food and drinks <u>such as</u> *croissants* (crescent rolls) and *latte* (coffee with milk).

► This happens even when two countries have the same language. <u>Take</u> the United States and England <u>for example</u>.

Practice

A. Find examples in "The Language of Food." Underline sentences with expressions that introduce examples. There are six expressions in the reading.

B. Match the following ideas from the article with their examples.

Idea	Example
_____ **1.** Food names sometimes hide their true meanings.	**a.** For example, *pasta* is about the same thing as the English word *noodles,* but English speakers often use the Italian word.
_____ **2.** Food words also differ from country to country, even when two countries have the same language.	**b.** For instance, if you want a soft drink in New England ask for a soda; in the Midwest, ask for a pop.
_____ **3.** Even within the same country, the words aren't always the same.	**c.** For example, American cowboys renamed beans *Arizona strawberries.*
_____ **4.** English speakers often use the foreign food name even if there is an English word for the same thing.	**d.** The English call the American *cookie* a *biscuit* for example.

Vocabulary

A. Here are some more words from "The Language of Food." Find them in the reading and circle them.

Noun	Verbs	Adjectives
Midwest	match invented renamed	popular expensive

B. Now use the words to fill in the blanks below.

1. Chef Mario changed the name of his restaurant to "Mario's Café." He _____ it because he didn't like the old name.

2. The restaurant has a new ice cream flavor. Chef Mario _____ it at his restaurant.

3. You need a lot of money to eat at Mario's new restaurant. It's _____ .

4. Mario uses many different colored plates at this new restaurant. They're nice, but they don't _____ .

5. Too many people go to Mario's Café. Now we can't get a table at Mario's. It's too _____ .

6. Mario gets the best beef. It comes from cattle from the _____ . Beef from the middle of the United States tastes great.

Talk About It

Discuss the following questions:
1. What other foreign food names do you know in the English language?
2. Describe to your group members some interesting or strange foods or food words.

What other foreign food names do you know?

I think *wasabi* is used in English.

Expressions

Combining Verbs and Prepositions

In English, verbs are often combined with prepositions. Here are some examples:

> <u>Look at</u> the menu.   <u>Forget about</u> the soup.

There are no rules about the preposition to use; you just have to memorize the combinations. Use them frequently to help yourself learn them.

Practice

A. Find these verb + preposition combinations in *"Soup du Jour"* or "The Language of Food" and underline them in the readings.

> ask for   depending on   forget about   look at   mixed with

B. Now use the verb + preposition combinations to complete the following sentences.

1.   If you want a submarine sandwich in New Orleans, _____

   _____ a *po'boy.*

2.   An egg cream is seltzer _____ _____

   milk and chocolate syrup.

3.   Please _____ _____ the menu and order

   your pizza.

4.   Food names change in the United States, _____

   _____ the region you're in.

5.   David told the server to _____ _____

   the *soup du jour.*

Internet Research

Using an Online Dictionary

Online dictionaries are very useful. Some online dictionaries are for particular types of words, like food words. To find a food word online, go to a food website such as foodtv.com or epicurious.com. Type the word that you want to know into the text box. Then click the Search button.

Example:

When you click "Go," you'll get a definition. For compound food words such as "cake flour," use the base word, "flour." The definition might include all types of flour, so look for the exact term (**cake flour**). It's usually in **bold** type.

Practice

Look up some food words. Use an online food dictionary or use a food website such as www.foodtv.com or www.epicurious.com. Use your own ideas or the following words from a cake recipe.

► cake flour
► heavy cream
► to sift
► vanilla extract
► tube pan
► to cream (butter)

Tell the class whether or not you found the word, how you found it, and what it means.

Write About It

A. Write the following paragraphs. Fill in the blanks. Write complete sentences.

Paragraph One

Because different foods grow at different times of the year, there are summer foods and

winter foods. An example of a summer food is _____ . This is

[Write a summer food]

_____ .

[Describe the food]

An example of a winter food is _____ . It's _____

[Write a winter food]   [Describe the food]

_____ .

Paragraph Two

Some things are easy to cook. For instance, _____ is easy to

[Write a food that is easy to cook]

cook because _____ .

[Explain why it's easy to cook]

Some things are difficult to cook. Take for example _____ . It's

[Write a food that is difficult to cook]

difficult to cook because _____ .

[Explain why it's difficult to cook]

B. Now write your own paragraphs. First, write a paragraph about summer and winter foods. Then write another about foods that are easy or difficult to cook. Try to include four new words or expressions from this chapter in your paragraphs.

C. Write more paragraphs about food. Here are some ideas:
- ▶ Write a review of the food at your favorite restaurant.
- ▶ Describe a time when you had trouble ordering food in a restaurant.
- ▶ Answer this question: What is the strangest food you ever ate and why did you eat it?
- ▶ Compare food words in different countries or regions.
- ▶ Describe a time you tried a new food.
- ▶ Your own idea

Include three new words or expressions from this chapter in your paragraphs. Also, try to use your Internet research.

On Your Own

Project

Take a survey. Ask your classmates about food.

Step 1: Practice

Listen as your teacher reads the food survey questions below. Do you understand them? Repeat them after your teacher so you can pronounce them correctly.

Step 2: Take a Survey

Ask five classmates questions about food. Indicate *M* (male) or *F* (female) for each person. Use one copy of the form for each classmate.

Food Survey

Name _____   M _____   F _____

1. What do you call these items? (List three foods.)

   _____ : _____
   [food]
   _____ : _____
   [food]
   _____ : _____
   [food]

2. What do you call the three meals of the day?

   _____

   _____

3. How many meals do you eat on Sunday? What do you call them?

   _____

   _____

4. Where are you from?

   _____

Step 3: Follow-Up

Explain the results of your survey to the class.

Wrap Up

How Much Do You Remember?

Check your new knowledge. In this chapter, you learned facts, words, and expressions. You also learned reading skills and you practiced writing. Complete the following to check what you remember.

1. What is *soup du jour*?

_____

2. List two foreign food names that English speakers use.

_____

3. Give another name for *soda*.

_____

4. Write a sentence with a verb + preposition combination from one of your paragraphs.

_____

5. What did you learn from your survey?

_____

6. Give a new food word and its meaning from your Internet research.

_____

Second Timed Readings

Now reread *"Soup du Jour"* and "The Language of Food." Time each reading separately. Write your times for all the Timed Readings in this chapter in the Timed Reading Chart on page 213.

Crossword Puzzle

Complete the crossword puzzle to practice some words and expressions from this chapter.

CLUES

Across →
3. Milk _____ _____ ice cream makes a milk shake.
5. An Italian word for *noodles*
7. A big sandwich in New England
8. A soft drink in the Midwest

Down ↓
1. The soup of the day
2. Cowboys used to eat Arizona _____.
4. _____ _____ where you live, food names are different.
6. If you want help, just _____ _____ it.

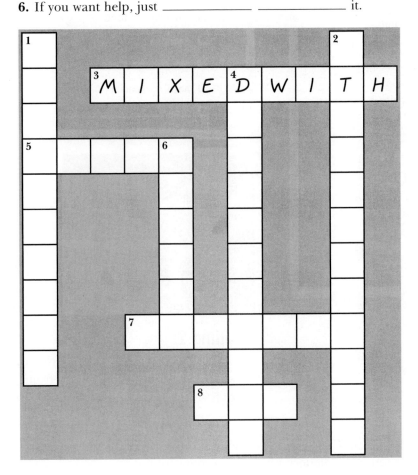

Food and Health

CHAPTER PREVIEW

In this chapter, you'll:

Content
▶ read a timeline of nutrition advice from 3200 B.C. to the present
▶ discover how modern research is studying ancient ideas about food and health

Reading Skills
▶ use topic, title, and headings to preview the main idea and the supporting details
▶ take notes on a reading to help you remember important information

Vocabulary Skills
▶ use words and expressions to talk about health problems
▶ use expressions to discuss health benefits and advice

Writing Skills
▶ write about healthy foods and eating habits

Research Skills
▶ identify valid sources of information on the Internet
▶ interview people about their opinions of traditional and modern medicine

The rest of the world lives to eat while I eat to live. 🐌

—Socrates
(Greek philosopher, 469–399 B.C.)

SHORT SURVEY

I do the following to stay healthy:
❑ take vitamins
❑ eat healthy food
❑ exercise
❑ get enough sleep
❑ nothing special
❑ other _____

Reading 1:
Is chocolate good for you? Can eating cabbage cure warts? Read nutrition advice from 3200 B.C. to the present.

Reading 2:
What did the ancient Chinese believe about ginger? Were they right? Read about modern research on some ancient ideas about food and health.

What do you think?

Write ten things in the box that you ate and drank yesterday.

_____	_____	_____
_____	_____	_____
_____	_____	_____
_____		

Why did you eat or drink these things? Put each item from the box above into one of the categories below. Some items can go into more than one column.

I was hungry/ thirsty.	It tasted good.	It was healthy.	Someone gave it to me.	I didn't have time to make anything else.	Other _____ _____ _____ _____

Compare your list with a partner. Then discuss the following questions:

1. How often do you eat healthy food? What do you eat?
2. How often do you eat unhealthy food? What do you eat?

Reading 1: Nutrition "Dos and Don'ts" for 5,200 Years

Before You Read

Preview

A. The title of Reading 1 is "Nutrition 'Dos and Don'ts' for 5,200 Years." What do you think it's about? Discuss with a partner.

B. Look at the following list of eating and drinking habits. In your opinion, which ones are good for you? Which ones are bad for you? Which ones are neither good nor bad? Write *G* (Good), *B* (Bad) or *N* (Neither) next to each item.

_____ eating pork (meat from a pig)	_____ drinking hot drinks
_____ eating chocolate	_____ eating cold foods
_____ drinking cold drinks	_____ eating low-fat foods
_____ eating cabbage	_____ drinking coffee or tea
_____ eating low calorie foods	_____ eating sweet foods
_____ eating uncooked (raw) foods	_____ not eating meat
_____ eating fast	_____ eating fast food (e.g., from Burger King)
_____ eating slowly	
_____ drinking milk	_____ chewing food a long time before swallowing
_____ eating animal fats (e.g., butter, cheese)	

C. Compare and discuss your answers with a partner. Give a reason for your opinion.

I think eating animal fats is bad for you because . . .

Really? I think . . .

Vocabulary

A. Preview words from Reading 1. Use the words to complete the sentences below.

> ancient   antioxidants   brittle   Carbohydrates
> conquered   nutrition   reincarnation   timid

1. This diet book is very old. In fact, it's _____. Someone wrote it before the year 1 A.D.

2. Some people believe in _____. They believe that after they die, they will be born again.

3. He should not play sports because his bones are very _____. They can break easily.

4. Mimi is afraid to speak in class because she is very _____.

5. A long time ago, the Romans fought and _____ the people in Britain. The Romans came to their land, took it from them, and told the people how to live.

6. _____ can give you energy. They are in foods such as fruits, vegetables, and grains.

7. The science of _____ helps us know what to eat and drink for good health.

8. Many food scientists tell us to eat foods with _____. These are chemicals in food that can help keep the body healthy.

B. Now scan the passage "Nutrition 'Dos and Don'ts' For 5,200 Years" on pages 70–71 for the three words below. Underline the words within the passage. Then read the sentences before and after them. Can you find definitions for the words in the sentences that are around them? Circle the definitions. Then write each definition next to the correct word.

corpulence: _____

fasted: _____

vegetarian: _____

As You Read

As you read, think about this question:

▶ Did people in the past have the same ideas about nutrition as we do today?

> The only way to keep your health is to eat what you don't want, drink what you don't like and do what you'd druther [rather] not. 🍵
>
> —*Mark Twain*
> *(American author, 1835–1910)*

🎧 Nutrition "Dos and Don'ts" for 5,200 Years

Today, many people are interested in nutrition. They want to know what to eat for good health. This was also true thousands of years ago. Here is some interesting nutrition advice from the past:

3200 B.C.

5   According to Louis E. Grivetti, an expert on ancient diets, people in the north of Egypt ate pork before 3200 B.C. People in the south of Egypt didn't eat pork. Shortly after 3200 B.C., people in the south conquered the north. Then no one in ancient Egypt ate pork.

EGYPT

c. 500 B.C.

10   Pythagoras, the ancient Greek mathematician, was a vegetarian. He was a vegetarian because he believed in reincarnation. He believed that not eating meat meant that you never ate your relatives.

175 B.C.

Cato, a Roman politician, said that eating cabbage keeps you well. According to Cato, cabbage cures stomachaches and warts.

1361

15   The Chinese physician Hua Shou wrote about eating and health. He believed that bad eating habits led to bad health. For example, he said, "Do not drink cold liquids when you are cold and do not eat too much. This can keep you healthy."

Cabbage

1600s

The English author Francis Quarles fasted (ate nothing) occasionally to be healthy.

1630s

20   The Seneca Indians played a sport similar to lacrosse. The players of this sport ate special foods. They believed that not eating certain animals would make them better players. For example, they didn't eat frogs before playing. Frogs, they said, had brittle bones. They also didn't eat rabbits before playing. The rabbits, they said, were timid.

1864

In 1864, William Banting published the first known diet book: "Letter on Corpulence" (being fat). Banting said, "Eat low carbohydrate foods." Banting became frightened about his weight because he could no longer tie his shoes. The diet book was very popular. More than 58,000 copies were sold.

1910s

Horace Fletcher said for best health, chew your food at least 32 times. Then swallow. This was called "Fletcherism."

1941

In 1941, the U.S. government wrote the first set of Recommended Dietary Allowances (RDA). The RDA says what nutrients every person should eat every day for "perfect health."

2000

A study found that one in four people feel better after they eat chocolate. Other studies show the health benefits of chocolate. For example, it has antioxidants—chemicals in food that keep the body healthy.

Word Count: 394

Timed Reading

Read "Nutrition 'Dos and Don'ts' for 5,200 Years" again. Read at a comfortable speed. Time your reading.

Start time: _____

End time: _____

My reading time: _____

After You Read

Comprehension

A. Which of these statements is not true? Fill in the bubble for the correct answer.

- (A) People in the past were interested in food and health.
- (B) People in the past didn't think that food was important for health.
- (C) Some people in the past believed that eating cabbage kept you well.

B. Fill in the bubble for each correct answer.

1. Before 3200 B.C., _____ ate pork.

- (A) Northern Egyptians
- (B) Southern Egyptians
- (C) no one in Egypt

2. What did the Chinese physician Hua Shou believe?

- (A) It is important to think about the temperature of liquids that you drink.
- (B) You should only drink cold liquids when you are cold.
- (C) When you are cold, you should not drink cold liquids.

3. What did the Seneca Indians believe about food and sports?

- (A) Eating frogs and rabbits made them better players.
- (B) Not eating frogs and rabbits made them better players.
- (C) Lacrosse players don't have to think about food.

4. Which statement about William Banting is true?

- (A) He thought that carbohydrates were good for you.
- (B) He was worried about his weight.
- (C) No one bought his diet book.

5. Studies of chocolate show that _____.

- (A) it keeps the body healthy
- (B) it makes people feel good
- (C) both A and B

Reading 2: Foods That are Good for You

Reading Skills

Review: Using Topic, Titles, and Headings to Predict

In Chapter 1, you used personal experience to connect with a topic. In Chapters 2 and 3, you used titles and headings to predict main ideas and details. Good readers use all three to prepare for a reading before they read it. Here are the steps:

1. Read the title. Think about the main idea of the reading. Go beyond the main idea and guess details.

2. Think about the topic. Connect it to your experiences. Ask questions. Think about what you already know about the topic.

3. Read the section headings. Decide what each section is about.

4. Finally, put it all together and predict supporting details.

Practice

Practice using topic, title, and headings to make predictions. Look at "Foods That are Good for You" on pages 75–76. Look only at the title and headings. Work with a partner and answer the questions.

1. The topic of the reading passage is foods that can help cure or prevent disease. What questions can you ask yourself to connect to the topic?

   _____

2. Look at the title. What do you think the reading passage might be about?

   _____

3. Look at the heading for the first section. What do you think the first section might be about?

   _____

4. Look at the heading for the second section. What do you think the second section might be about?

   _____

5. Look at the heading for the third section. What do you think the third section might be about?

_____

6. Now predict: What do you think the main idea and supporting ideas of this reading are?

_____

_____

_____

Preview

A. The title of Reading 2 is "Foods That are Good for You." What do you think it's about? Discuss with a partner.

B. Here are some health condition words from the reading. Match them with the correct definitions on the right. Write the letter of the definition next to the correct word.

_____ arthritis		**a.**	infection caused by a virus
_____ cancer		**b.**	reddening and swelling of cells
_____ fever		**c.**	pain in the head
_____ flu		**d.**	sore or stiff joints
_____ headache		**e.**	pain in the throat
_____ inflammation		**f.**	abnormally high body temperature
_____ sore throat		**g.**	a lump or growth on or in the body
_____ tumor		**h.**	uncontrolled cell growth that keeps organs and body parts from working properly

As you read, think about this question:

▶ Which ancient ideas about healthy foods
  may be true today?

🎧 Foods That are Good for You

There is an American saying in English: "An apple a day keeps the doctor away." Many people agree that some foods are important for health. In fact, certain foods, spices, and herbs are a part of *traditional* or *folk medicine*. Traditional medicine is medicine that is not based on modern science. In ancient times,
5 people ate foods such as garlic and grapes for health, and they still do today. Some people might think that these ideas are just superstitions. However, modern science is proving the health benefits of many of these ordinary foods.

Foods in Traditional Medicine

Ancient documents talk about the use of foods, spices,
10 and herbs as medicine. For example, ancient Egyptian writings from 1500 B.C. mention garlic. They recommend garlic for headaches. The ancient Romans knew about the benefits of garlic, too. Around 110 A.D., the Roman writer Pliny wrote that garlic cured over 60 illnesses.

Garlic

15 Another important food in traditional medicine is grapes. The ancient Romans believed that grapes and raisins (dried grapes) cured many illnesses. Some people drank grape juice for sore throats. Other people used raisins for stomach problems. Some people even believed that grapes helped to heal tumors (lumps or growths in or on the body).

20 Ginger is another healthy food in ancient and traditional medicine. People used ginger over 2,500 years ago for many health problems. Confucius, the Chinese philosopher, wrote about it in the fifth century, B.C. Traditional Chinese medicine prescribes ginger for stomach problems, sore throats, fever, and flu. Ginger is also used in
25 an ancient system of medicine from India (Ayurvedic medicine). In this system, ginger is used to treat arthritis.

Ginger

Current Research

Why are certain foods good for you? Ancient people knew that they were good. However, they didn't know *why* they were good. Modern researchers are studying many of these foods and finding them high in healthy compounds.

30 Some of these compounds are called antioxidants. Antioxidants keep cells healthy. For example, the National Cancer Institute is studying garlic. They are finding that garlic contains antioxidants. The antioxidants in garlic help to protect cells, so researchers think that eating garlic might prevent cancer. Researchers in China are also studying garlic. They found a similar result: peo-

35 ple who ate garlic were 60 percent less likely to get stomach cancer.

Researchers at Columbia University College of Physicians and Surgeons in New York are studying a compound in grapes. These researchers think that this compound might also prevent cancer. And scientists at Tufts University are studying the antioxidants in raisins; these antioxidants seem to remove *free radicals* in the

40 blood. Free radicals are compounds that can cause cell damage. So eating grapes and raisins might also keep you healthy.

Research is showing that ginger can reduce pain and inflammation—the reddening and swelling of cells. Researchers at the University of Sydney, Australia, are studying a compound in ginger. This compound reduces pain and

45 inflammation like aspirin, but it is even better. Aspirin can upset the stomach, but ginger calms the stomach.

Learning from Traditional Medicine

Researchers are also studying other ordinary foods and drinks such as nuts, blueberries, cold-water fish, cocoa, and tea. They are finding that these foods have many beneficial compounds. Modern medicine is learning from traditional

50 medicine, and so can we.

Word Count: 551

Timed Reading

Read the "Foods That are Good for You" again. Read at a comfortable speed. Time your reading.

Start time: _____

End time: _____

My reading time: _____

After You Read

Main Idea

What is the main idea of "Foods That are Good for You"? Fill in the bubble for the correct answer.

- (A) Traditional medicine is not based on modern science.
- (B) Compounds in ginger, garlic, and grapes can help cure disease.
- (C) Modern science is learning that many ideas from traditional medicine may be true.

Look at your predictions from pages 73–74. Were they correct?

Getting the Details

Both traditional and modern medicine believe that garlic, grapes, and ginger can cure or help prevent certain illnesses. Use the information in "Foods That are Good for You." Put each of the following illnesses in the correct column of the chart below. An illness may go in more than one column.

arthritis inflammation	cancer pain	fever sore throat	flu stomachache	headache tumors

Garlic	Grapes	Ginger

Reading Skills

Making Notes as You Read

Good readers make notes as they read. They make notes about the information in the reading passage. This helps them to pay attention and to remember important information.

There are many ways to makes notes as you read. Here are some ideas:

▶ Write in the margins (the white spaces around the passage) your questions about the reading, things that you agree or disagree with, ideas that you can connect with, or items you want more information on. Draw lines from your notes to words in the passage.

▶ Circle, mark with a star (*), or draw a box around important dates and numbers, or words that you don't know.

Example:

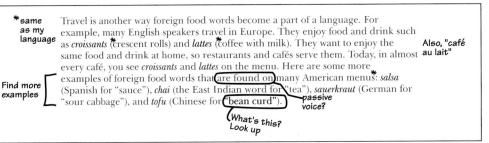

Practice

Read "Foods That are Good for You" again. As you read, write notes in the margins. Circle, box, or mark with a star numbers, dates, and words. Draw lines from your notes to the numbers, dates, and words. Make notes on the following:

▶ information that answers the pre-reading question

▶ ideas that you agree or disagree with

▶ questions you have about the information in the passage

▶ what you still want to know about the topic

Compare your notes with a partner's notes.

Vocabulary

A. Here are some more words and expressions from "Foods That are Good for You." Find them in the reading passage and circle them.

Nouns	Verbs	Adjective
compounds superstitions traditional (or folk) medicine	cured reduce	beneficial

B. Now use them to complete the sentences.

1. If you bump your knee, cold water can _____ the swelling. This works because cold temperatures make things smaller.

2. Ancient people had many _____ about health, but some of these unscientific beliefs may be true.

3. Cocoa can be very _____ for your health because it contains things that are good for you, such as antioxidants.

4. Many beliefs from _____ _____

   _____ _____ might be true. Scientists are studying many of these ancient ideas about health.

5. The doctor _____ Jack's skin problem. He used a new medicine and Jack's skin problem quickly improved.

6. Combinations of chemicals in grapes are good for health. These _____ might prevent cancer.

Talk About It

Discuss the following questions:

What other foods help to cure disease? Give the food or drink and the disease or problem that it helps to cure. Are these ideas from traditional medicine, modern science, or both?

Expressions

Talking about Health Beliefs and Advice

Here are some verb combinations. They help you talk about cures for conditions.
Note: "X" is the cure; "Y" is the condition.

X cures/cured Y   X helps to heal Y   X is used for Y
X might prevent Y   prescribes X for Y   use X for Y
X keeps/can keep you well/healthy   X is used to treat Y

Examples:
Ginger is used to treat arthritis.
  cure   condition

Traditional Chinese medicine prescribes ginger for stomach problems.
                                       cure   condition

Cabbage cures stomachaches.
  cure   condition

Practice

A. Find and underline the expressions in "Nutrition 'Dos and Don'ts' for 5,200 Years" or "Foods That are Good for You."

B. Now complete the following sentences using the expressions and the information from the reading passages. (You can also look at the cures and conditions in the chart you made on page 77 for ideas.) More than one phrase can be correct in each sentence.

Example: Modern science thinks that <u>garlic might prevent cancer</u>.

1. Current research is finding that ———————————————————————.

2. The ancient Romans believed that ————————————————————.

3. In Ayurvedic medicine, ————————————————————————.

4. Researchers think that —————————————————————————.

5. Cato, a Roman politician, said that ——————————————————.

6. Research is showing that ————————————————————————.

Internet Research

Identifying Sources

When you do an Internet search, you often get several results. Some might be useful and some might not. How can you tell? You look at the URL, or website address. Website addresses usually show the name of a person or organization. In addition, most end with one of the following: .com, .edu, .gov, or .org.

The ending .com is usually for a business such as a store; .edu is used for an educational institution, such as a university; .gov is used for government agencies; and .org is usually for a nonprofit organization, such as a charity. Always read the entire URL to decide if the result might be useful.

For example, you want to know about the latest research on the health benefits of blueberries. You get these URLs among your results:
- www.vankleysblueberries.**com**/health.htm
- www.tufts.**edu**/communications.html

Which website should you visit first? Probably the Tufts website because universities do research studies. Vankley's Blueberries is probably a store. If it has scientific information about products, it may not be as detailed as information from a university.

Practice

Practice reading URLs to evaluate search results. Do a search for the following:

1. Try to find the latest research on the health benefits of chocolate. Look at the URLs on the first page of your results.

2. Pick one or two that you think have the best information.

3. Go to the websites and check them. Were you right?

4. Check some that you don't think are useful by going to those websites. Were you right?

5. Print your search results page. Circle the useful URLs and underline the ones that weren't useful.

6. Bring the page to class to compare and discuss your experience.

Write About It

A. Write the following paragraphs. Fill in the blanks. Write complete sentences.

Paragraph One

I commonly eat three foods that researchers say are good for my health. One is

_____ . It is healthy because _____
[Write the name of a healthy food]   [Explain why]

_____ . Another food that is healthy is _____ .
                                                                    [Write the name of the food]

It's good for me because it _____
                                    [Explain why]

_____ is also a healthy food. It's healthy because _____
[Write the name of a healthy food]   [Explain why]

_____ .

Paragraph Two

In my opinion, _____ is bad for your health. It's bad because
                    [Write a bad eating habit]

_____ . Another eating
                            [Explain why]

habit that isn't healthy is _____ . This is unhealthy because
                                [Write a bad eating habit]

_____ .
                            [Explain why]

B. Now write your own paragraphs. First, write a paragraph about three foods that are
good for you. Then write another one about two eating habits that are bad for health.
Try to include four new words and expressions from this chapter in your paragraphs.

C. Write more paragraphs about food and health. Here are some ideas:
   ▶ Describe a traditional food from your country or culture.
   ▶ List three things you could do to improve your eating habits?
   ▶ Give advice to someone who has one of these conditions: a headache, a cold, or a sore throat.

Include four words or expressions from this chapter in your paragraphs. Also, try to use
your Internet research.

On Your Own

Project

Take a survey. Ask your classmates about their ideas on medicine.

Step 1: Practice

Listen as your teacher reads the medicine survey below. Do you understand the three choices in question 1? Repeat the question with your teacher so you can pronounce it correctly.

Step 2: Take a Survey

Ask five classmates the question about medicine. Indicate *M* (male) or *F* (female) for each person. Use one copy of the form below for each classmate.

Medicine Survey

Name _____   M _____   F _____

1. Which of the following is best, in your opinion?
   _____ traditional medicine
   _____ modern medicine
   _____ a combination of traditional and modern medicine
   (Choose one)
2. Explain your opinion.
   _____
   _____
   _____

Step 3: Follow-Up

Explain the results of your survey to the class. For example, "I asked five people the question. Two people said that, in their opinion, traditional medicine is the best. Three said that a combination of traditional and modern medicine is the best."

How Much Do You Remember?

Check your new knowledge. In this chapter, you learned facts, words, and expressions. You also learned reading skills and you practiced writing. Complete the following to check what you remember.

1. Give an example of health advice from ancient times.

   _____

2. Explain what modern science is finding out about garlic, ginger, or grapes.

   _____

3. Use *compounds* in a sentence.

   _____

4. Rewrite your answer to Question 2. Use an expression to give health advice.

   _____

5. What did you learn from your survey?

   _____

6. What does *.edu* in an Internet address mean?

   _____

Second Timed Readings

Now reread "Nutrition 'Dos and Don'ts' for 5,200 Years" and "Foods That are Good for You." Time each reading separately. Write your times for all the Timed Readings from this chapter in the Timed Reading Chart on page 213.

Crossword Puzzle

Complete the crossword puzzle to practice some words from this chapter.

CLUES

Across ➜
5. Not eating meat
7. These are in pasta, rice, and bread.
8. The Roman writer Pliny wrote that garlic _____ over 60 illnesses.

Down ↓
1. Ginger, garlic, and grapes are _____ foods because they can keep you healthy.
2. Being born again
3. Traditional Chinese medicine _____ ginger for sore throats.
4. The opposite of *modern*
6. Combinations of chemicals

Physics and History of Sports

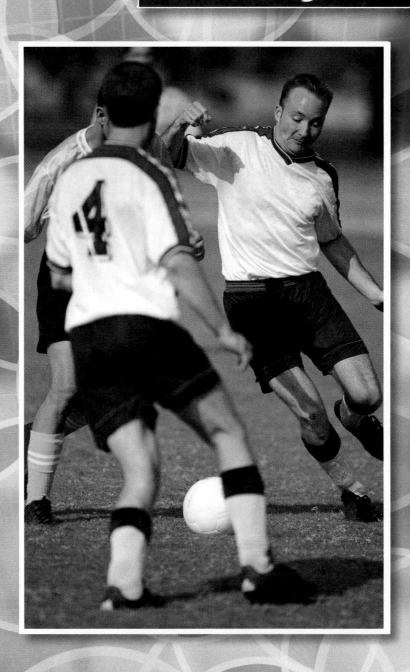

What is Physics?

Science is often divided into two areas: physical science and life science. Physics is one of the physical sciences. Physics has many different areas. Some of them are

- energy
- heat
- matter
- forces
- light
- motion
- sound

The father of physics is Thales of Miletus. He predicted an eclipse in 585 B.C. and believed that everything was made of water. Democritus lived between 460 and 370 B.C. He named the atom.

SOME FAMOUS PHYSICISTS

Some famous physicists include:

Ibn-al-Haytham—Persian, 965–1040

Nicolaus Copernicus—Polish, 1473–1543

Galileo Galilei—Italian, 1564–1642

Johannes Kepler—German, 1571–1630

Isaac Newton—English, 1643-1727

Marie Curie—French, 1867–1934

Albert Einstein—German-American, 1879–1955

Niels Bohr—Danish, 1885–1962

Richard Feynman—American, 1918–1988

Stephen Hawking—English, 1942–

Physics and You

Physics is helpful in careers such as engineering, medicine, space exploration, computer science, and industry.

Do you want to study physics? Ask yourself these questions:

- Am I curious about how things work?
- Do I like to think about problems and solutions?
- Do I like to do experiments?
- Do I like mathematics?

5 The Physics of Sports

CHAPTER PREVIEW

In this chapter, you'll:

Content
▶ read questions and answers about sports and science
▶ read about athletes and the laws of physics

Reading Skills
▶ preview the ideas in a reading by using pictures
▶ outline a reading to help you remember what you read

Vocabulary Skills
▶ use words and expressions for talking about sports and the laws of physics
▶ use expressions with *go* to describe movement

Writing Skills
▶ write about sports and physics

Research Skills
▶ learn how to find images on the Internet
▶ interview people about the sports they like

> Statistically, 100% of the shots you don't take don't go in. 🐌
>
> —*Wayne Gretzky (Canadian hockey player, b. 1961)*

SHORT SURVEY

Which sports do you like to play or watch?

❑ baseball
❑ basketball
❑ tennis
❑ soccer
❑ swimming
❑ other _____

Reading 1:

Why do golf balls have dimples? Read "Sports Q & A" to find out.

Reading 2:

How do soccer players use Newton's first law? Read about athletes and the laws of physics to find out.

What do you think?

How interested are you in sports? Answer the questions in the chart below. Then work with a partner. Ask your partner the questions. Compare your answers.

How many days a week do you participate in sports?

I usually ...

Sports, Exercise, and You

Circle your answers to the following questions.

Participating:

1. How often do you participate in sports?

Daily   1 time a week   2–3 times a week   4–6 times a week   Never

2. Do you prefer an individual sport, like running or swimming, or a team sport such as soccer or baseball?

Individual   Team

3. Are you a member of a sports team?

Yes   No

If yes, for which sport(s)?_____

Watching:

4. How often do you watch sports?

Daily   1 time a week   2–3 times a week   4–6 times a week   Never

5. Do you like to watch individual or team sports?

Individual   Team

6. What sports do you like to watch? _____

7. Where do you watch sports?

At home   At a friend's house   In a public place   Other: _____

Reading 1: Sports Q & A

Before You Read

Preview

A. The title of Reading 1 is "Sports Q & A." What do you think it's about? (Hint: Think about what *Q* and *A* usually mean when they are together like this.) Discuss with a partner.

B. Look at these pictures. What is happening in each one? Discuss with a partner.

1.

2.

3.

4.

C. Now discuss these questions with your partner:

1. Which of these sports have you seen in real life? On TV? In movies?

2. Which of these sports do you do?

Which of these sports do you do?

I golf.

Vocabulary

A. Below is a list of sports equipment. Read the list and then write each piece of equipment in the correct column. There are two pieces of equipment for each sport. One is done for you.

arrow	backboard	bat	bathing cap	~~bow~~
golf club	hockey stick	home plate	hoop	lane dividers
puck	racket	tee	tennis ball	

Archery	Ice Hockey	Basketball	Golf	Baseball	Tennis	Swimming
bow						

B. Now go back and try to add more pieces of equipment to the chart above.

As You Read

You are going to read and try to answer questions about sports and science. As you read the questions, think about the connections between sports and science. Also, try and picture in your mind what each sport, action, or piece of equipment looks like.

🎧 Sports Q & A

How much do you know about sports and science? Can you answer these questions yourself? If not, make a guess. Then read the next page to find out the answers.

1. Why does a golf ball have dimples (small indentations)?

2. When basketball players jump, they look as though they stay in the air a long time. Why?

3. Why do high jumpers go headfirst and backwards over the bar?

4. Why are there so many left-handed batters in baseball?

5. Do lane dividers help swimmers swim faster?

A high jumper

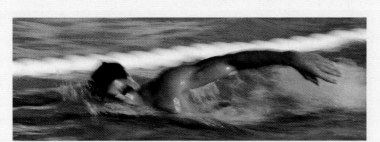

Lane divider and swimmer

A golf ball

ANSWERS

1. Golf balls were originally smooth. However, the ball goes farther with dimples. The dimples keep the air flowing over the golf ball longer. This makes the ball go farther.

2. They look like they stay in the air a long time because they bend their knees and pull their feet up. Also, they may hold on to the ball until they are coming down and then slam-dunk the ball.

3. They go higher. When high jumpers jump, they raise their center of gravity as high as they can. Before 1968, high jumpers went forward over the bar. They kept the center of gravity in their body. After 1968, high jumpers went backwards over the bar. Now they can go higher than their center of gravity and they can jump over higher bars.

4. There are many left-handed batters because they can get to first base faster. They stand two steps closer to first base. Therefore, they can get to first base faster than right-handed hitters can.

5. Yes. Swimmers swim fastest in smooth water. Lane dividers with disks break up the waves and make the water smoother. Then swimmers can swim faster.

Word Count: 329

Timed Reading

Read "Sports Q & A" again. Read at a comfortable speed. Time your reading.

Start time: _____

End time: _____

My reading time: _____

After You Read

Comprehension

A. How many questions from "Sports Q & A" did you answer correctly? As you were reading, did you see pictures in your mind?

B. Fill in the bubble for each correct answer.

1. Golf balls have dimples to make them _____.

   (A) easier to find   (B) go farther   (C) stay in one place

2. What makes basketball players look as though they stay in the air a long time?

   (A) They lift their arms to look as though they jumped higher.

   (B) Everyone is looking at the ball, so it only *feels* like a long time.

   (C) They bend their knees and pull up their feet.

3. When high jumpers go over the bar headfirst and backwards, their center of gravity _____ their body.

   (A) stays in   (B) is above   (C) is below

4. An advantage left-handed batters have in baseball is that they are _____.

   (A) two steps closer to first base   (B) on home plate

   (C) two steps closer to third base

5. What disadvantage do swimmers have in a pool without lane dividers?

   (A) The water is rougher.   (B) The water is colder.   (C) The water is hotter.

Talk About It

Discuss the following questions about "Sports Q & A."

1. What information was new to you? What did you know already?

2. Can you give any other examples of the connection between science and sports?

What was new to you?

I didn't know . . .

Reading 2: Athletes and the Laws of Physics

Before You Read

Reading Skills

Using Pictures to Understand Ideas

Photographs, diagrams, and drawings can help you understand new ideas in a reading passage. They often have captions (explanations). Captions give you even more information. If you look at photographs, diagrams, and drawings and their captions before you read, they will help you to predict what the reading is about. If you look at the pictures and captions as you read, they will help you understand the author's ideas.

The Frisbee keeps moving until someone catches it or it hits the ground.

For example, look at this idea: "An object in motion will stay in motion." Think about what it means. Now look at this picture and read the caption. It shows a man throwing a Frisbee. The picture and the caption explain the idea and make it easier to understand.

Note: In textbooks, photographs, diagrams, and drawings are often called **figures.**

Practice

Look at the figures in "Athletes and the Laws of Physics" on pages 97–98. They show Newton's Laws. Answer the questions and do the activities related to the figures.

1. In which section is Figure 1? Write the heading for that section.

_____

2. Look at Figure 1. Read the caption. Write the caption on the line.

_____

3. Now make a guess: What do you think Newton's First Law is?

_____

4. In which section is Figure 2? Write the heading for that section.

_____

5. Look at Figure 2. Read the caption. Write the caption on the line.

_____

6. Now make a guess: What do you think Newton's Second Law is?

_____

Preview

A. The title of Reading 2 is "Athletes and the Laws of Physics." What do you think it's about? Discuss with a partner.

B. Here are some words from the reading. Use them to complete the sentences below.

curb	force	ground
in motion	object	resists

1. Paul was skateboarding and didn't see the edge of the sidewalk. He fell off the

   _____ and broke his ankle.

2. When Nancy kicks the soccer ball, her kick is a(n) _____ on the ball. That means the energy from her kick makes the ball move.

3. Tina likes to run on the street and not the beach because the street _____ her weight. When she pushes down to run, the hard street stops the movement of her foot.

4. David is a great basketball player. On the court, he never stops running. In fact, he's always

   _____ _____.

5. Barry tried to catch the baseball before it hit the _____ because if it touched the earth, the batter would be safe at first base.

6. If you watch the movement of a(n) _____, such as a golf ball, a ping-pong ball, or a surfboard, you can learn how the laws of physics work.

As You Read

As you read, think about this question:
▶ Why are Newton's laws of physics important to athletes?

🎧 Athletes and the Laws of Physics

When you run fast, it's often hard to stop. Then when you stop, it's often hard to start again. Why? Sir Isaac Newton, the great seventeenth century scientist and mathematician, understood the reasons.

5　Newton described three laws of motion, and they are all important to athletes. They are important in soccer, baseball, running, and other sports. Let's look at these laws and see how they help athletes.

Sir Isaac Newton

Newton's First Law

Newton's first law says that an object in motion will stay in motion unless a force pushes it or pulls it. A soccer player uses this
10　law. The player kicks the ball. Then the ball moves. Often it gets kicked again. Then it changes direction. It stops if someone stops it. It also stops if it hits the net.

Figure 1: An object stops moving when a force (the net) pushes against it.

Newton's Second Law

Newton's second law says that if you push or pull an object, it goes in the direction of the force. A baseball player uses this law.
15　The baseball player hits the ball with a bat. The player hits the ball in a particular direction, such as to right field. The ball then travels in that direction.

Newton's second law also says that a heavy object needs more force to go fast than a light object does. A baseball weighs about
20　5.12 ounces (145 grams). If a baseball player hits a baseball with the bat, the ball travels at about 75 miles per hour (121 kph). A tennis ball weighs about 2 ounces (57 grams). What happens if the baseball player hits a tennis ball with the bat? The baseball player does not have to hit the tennis ball as hard for it to travel at the
25　same speed.

Figure 2: The baseball goes in the direction of the force.

Newton's Third Law

Newton's third law makes sports possible. It says that if you push or pull an object, it will push or pull back equally with the same force. How does this make sports possible? Let's look at runners. A runner's foot pushes against the ground. Usually the ground does
30 not move. It resists. That is, seems to push back. This push of the ground makes the runner go forward. The ground is very big, so the runner doesn't feel the push. Sometimes the ground is soft, for example, if it's muddy. What happens if the runner tries to run in mud? The ground doesn't resist right away. It doesn't push back
35 immediately. Then it's harder to run. Here's another example: running on the beach. Which is easier—running on hard sand or running on soft sand? All changes in motion follow this third law, even walking. When you walk, you push the ground. The ground resists, and this resistance helps you walk.

40 You can find examples of Newton's laws in all sports. They help a surfer ride a wave, a skateboarder jump over a curb, or a soccer player make a goal. Your favorite sports stars might not think too much about Newton when they play, but Newton's laws are helping them all the time.

Figure 3: The foot pushes the ground. The ground resists with enough force to prevent the foot from going down.

Word Count: 503

Timed Reading

Read "Athletes and the Laws of Physics" again. Read at a comfortable speed. Time your reading.

Start time: _____

End time: _____

My reading time: _____

After You Read

Main Idea

What is the main idea in "Athletes and the Laws of Physics"? Fill in the bubble of the correct answer.

(A) Athletes must study the laws of physics.

(B) The laws of physics help athletes.

(C) Baseball and soccer use the laws of physics.

Reading Skills

Outlining a Reading Passage

Outlining a reading passage is a good way to learn the information in it. Making an outline helps you find and remember the main ideas and the details in a reading passage. It also helps you organize the ideas so you can review them later. A traditional outline has the following format:

Title

Introduction: Main Idea
I.   Supporting Idea #1
    A. Specific Detail #1
    B. Specific Detail #2
II.   Supporting Idea #2
    A. Specific Detail #1
    B. Specific Detail #2
III. Supporting Idea #3
    A. Specific Detail #1
    B. Specific Detail #2
Conclusion

Look at the example on the next page. It's an outline of Reading 2 in Chapter 4.

<table>
<tr><td><u>Title</u></td><td>*Foods That are Good for You*</td></tr>
<tr><td>Introduction:</td><td>*Modern science is proving the health benefits of many ordinary foods.*</td></tr>
<tr><td>I. Supporting Idea # 1</td><td>*Ancient documents talk about the use of foods, spices, and herbs as medicine.*</td></tr>
<tr><td>A. Specific Detail #1</td><td>*Ancient Egyptians and Romans used garlic for headaches and other illnesses.*</td></tr>
<tr><td>B. Specific Detail #2</td><td>*Ancient Romans used grapes for sore throats, stomach problems, and tumors.*</td></tr>
<tr><td>C. Specific Detail #3</td><td>*Traditional Chinese and Indian medicine uses ginger for stomach problems, sore throats, fever, flu, and arthritis.*</td></tr>
<tr><td>II. Supporting Idea #2</td><td>*Modern researchers are studying these foods.*</td></tr>
<tr><td>A. Specific Detail #1</td><td>*Antioxidants in garlic help to protect cells, so might prevent cancer.*</td></tr>
<tr><td>B. Specific Detail #2</td><td>*Antioxidants in raisins may prevent cancer and get rid of free radicals in the blood.*</td></tr>
<tr><td>C. Specific Detail #3</td><td>*A compound in ginger can reduce pain and inflammation like aspirin.*</td></tr>
<tr><td>Conclusion:</td><td>*Modern medicine is learning from traditional medicine, and so can we.*</td></tr>
</table>

Practice

A. Go back to the reading "Athletes and the Laws of Physics." Use the headings to help you find the supporting ideas. Fill in the outline below.

Introduction (Main Idea): Three of Newton's Laws are important to athletes.

I. Supporting Idea #1 _____

_____

II. Supporting Idea #2 _____

_____

III. Supporting Idea #3 _____

_____

B. Now reread the passage and outline it completely on a separate piece of paper. Include the main idea, the supporting ideas, and specific details. Share your outline with a partner. Are the outlines alike?

Vocabulary

A. Here are some more words and expressions from "Athletes and the Laws of Physics." Find them in the reading passage and circle them.

> equally   grams   mph   mud   right field

B. Now use them to complete the sentences below.

1. Sometimes people write out the whole expression *miles per hour*, and sometimes they just use the short form, _____.

2. When it rains, dirt mixes with water and the ground gets wet and soft. This _____ makes running difficult.

3. Owen and Peter can both jump to the same height. They can jump _____ high.

4. If a baseball player hits the ball to the right, the ball will most likely land in _____ _____ .

5. Scientists use the metric system, so a scientist knows one ounce is 28.349 _____ .

Talk About It

Discuss the following questions about sports and physics:
1. What is your favorite sport to watch or play?
2. How does Newton's first law help you with your sport?
3. How does Newton's second law help you with your sport?
4. How does Newton's third law help you with your sport?
5. What else do you know about physics? How does your knowledge help you with your sport?

Expressions

Using *Go* to Describe Movement

The form *go* + adverb is very common in English. In these expressions, *go* means *move* or *travel* in a direction or in some way.

Examples:
High jumpers go headfirst over the bar.   A golf ball goes further with dimples.

A. Find and underline the following expressions in "Sports Q & A" or "Athletes and the Laws of Physics." (Note: Some expressions may be in figure captions and some may be in the answers.)

go as fast as	goes farther than	go headfirst
go higher than	goes faster than	goes in the direction of

B. Now use the expressions to complete the sentences below.

1. Michael is a great basketball player. When Michael jumps high in the air, he can

   _____ _____ _____ any other player.

2. Linda runs just like the other runners on the team. She can _____ _____

   _____ _____ anyone on her team.

3. Sue is not like the other runners on the team. She's faster. In fact, she _____

   _____ _____ anyone on her team.

4. Bill can run a long distance. He _____ _____ _____ anyone I know.

5. Sam, a high jumper, puts his head over the bar first. He learned to _____

   _____ from his teacher.

6. James taught his little brother to play soccer. James explained, "When you kick the ball, it

   _____ _____ _____ _____ _____ your kick."

Internet Research

Finding Images

Images (pictures, photos, and diagrams) help you understand ideas. You can find images easily on the Internet. To find an image on the Internet, go to a search site, such as Google (www.google.com), and click on "Images." Then type into the textbox keywords that describe the image that you want to see.

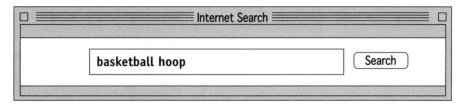

When searching for images, use the same keyword search skills that you practiced in Chapters 1–4.

Practice

A. Practice looking for images on the Internet. Try to find pictures that show the items on the list below. Print the best images and bring them to class.

- ▶ a hockey stick
- ▶ Newton's third law
- ▶ slam-dunk
- ▶ riding a wave
- ▶ your choice

B. Tell the class about your search experience. Talk about the images that you found. Explain how you found them. For example, what keywords did you use?

Write About It

A. Write paragraphs. Fill in the blanks. Write complete sentences.

Paragraph One

I like to watch/play _____
[Circle one]   [Write the name of a sport]

because _____.
[Explain the reason]

I also like to watch/play _____
[Circle one]   [Write the name of a sport]

because _____.
[Explain the reason]

Paragraph Two

Newton's laws of physics help in many sports. One example is _____.
[Write a sport]

Newton's _____ law helps players in this sport because
[Write the number of the law]

_____.
[Explain how the law helps players]

Newton's laws also help in _____. Newton's _____ law
[Write a sport]   [Write the number of the law]

helps players in this sport because _____.
[Explain how the law helps players]

B. Now write your own paragraphs. First, write a paragraph about watching or playing sports. Then write another about how the laws of physics help in sports. Try to include four new words or expressions from this chapter.

C. Write more paragraphs about sports and science. Here are some ideas:
  ▶ Answer these questions: How can you get better at a sport that you like? What can you do? Can the laws of physics help you get better?
  ▶ Explain why you *don't* like to watch or play certain sports.
  ▶ Find an image on the Internet that shows an athlete using one of Newton's laws. Write about the law being used and how the athlete is using it.

Include four new words or expressions from this chapter in your paragraphs. Also, try to use your Internet research.

On Your Own

Project

Design a survey. Ask your classmates about their favorite sports.

Step 1: Practice

With a partner, design a survey about sports. Think of three questions. Write your questions in the survey box below. Have your teacher check them to make sure that they are correct. Repeat the questions with your teacher so you can pronounce them correctly.

Sports Survey

1. Question: _____

Person 1   M _____   F _____ Answer: _____

Person 2   M _____   F _____ Answer: _____

Person 3   M _____   F _____ Answer: _____

2. Question: _____

Person 1   Answer: _____

Person 2   Answer: _____

Person 3   Answer: _____

3. Question: _____

Person 1   Answer: _____

Person 2   Answer: _____

Person 3   Answer: _____

Step 2: Take a Survey

Ask three classmates questions about sports. Indicate *M* (male) or *F* (female) for each person. Use the form above.

Step 3: Follow-Up

Explain the results of your survey to the class. For example, you could say, "I asked three people about the sports they play. Two people said that they don't play *any* sports. I was surprised because...."

How Much Do You Remember?

Check your knowledge. In this chapter, you learned facts, words, and expressions. You also learned reading skills and you practiced writing. Complete the following to check what you remember.

1. Why do golf balls have dimples?

   _____

2. Why do basketball players look as though they stay in the air a long time?

   _____

3. What is one of Newton's laws?

   _____

4. Use *go higher than* in a sentence.

   _____

5. How do you find images on the Internet?

   _____

6. Write one thing that you learned about your classmates from your survey.

   _____

Second Timed Readings

Now reread "Sports Q & A" and "Athletes and the Laws of Physics." Time each reading separately. Write the times for all the Timed Readings in this chapter in the Timed Reading Chart on page 214.

Crossword Puzzle

Complete the crossword puzzle to practice some words and expressions from this chapter.

CLUES

Across →
1. They're both good runners. They run _____ fast.
4. High jumpers _____ _____ over the bar.
6. Good soccer players don't stop moving. They're always _____ _____.
8. The edge of the sidewalk

Down ↓
2. These help swimmers swim faster.
3. When the ground doesn't move, it _____.
5. These make golf balls go farther.
7. A thing

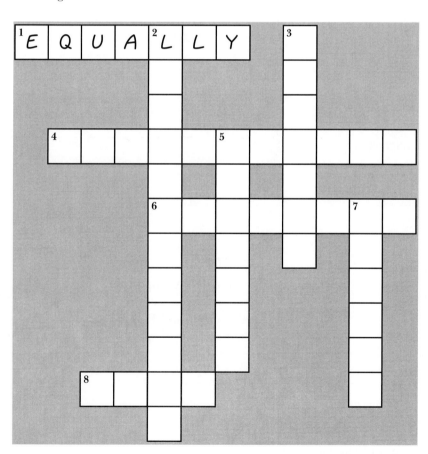

Sports History

CHAPTER PREVIEW

In this chapter, you'll:

Content
▶ read about the first person to run a four-minute mile
▶ read about the history of lacrosse and Benjamin Franklin's sports inventions

Reading Skills
▶ interact with a passage before you read it
▶ predict questions for a test

Vocabulary Skills
▶ use words and expressions to talk about the history of sports
▶ use expressions of age and time

Writing Skills
▶ write about sports and sports inventions

Research Skills
▶ find biographies on the Internet
▶ interview people about their sports history

> History is something that never happened, written by someone who wasn't there. ❧
>
> —*Gomez de la Serna (Spanish writer, 1888–1963)*

SHORT SURVEY

What are your favorite subjects in school?

❑ English

❑ history

❑ mathematics

❑ physical education

❑ science

❑ other _____

Reading 2:
Why is a dentist important in the history of lacrosse? Read "Sports and History" to find out.

Reading 1:
How did friends help Roger Bannister run a mile in less than four minutes? Read "The First Mile Under Four Minutes" to find out.

What do you think?

What's the best way to improve at a sport or other activity such as playing an instrument? Think about a time when you tried to improve at a sport or other activity. Look at the following strategies (plans). Which worked? Check (✓) *No* or *Yes* next to each strategy. If you check *Yes,* give a brief example of when you used that strategy.

Strategies	No	Yes	Example
1. I asked friends to show me how they do it.			
2. I got better equipment.			
3. I took lessons from a private coach or teacher.			
4. I read a book about it.			
5. I spent more time practicing.			
6. I took additional lessons.			
7. I stopped doing it for a while and then tried it again later.			
8. I visualized (imagined) doing it well.			
9. I watched others who do it well.			
10. Other_____			

Compare your answers with a partner. Then discuss the following questions:
What activity did you try to improve? Which strategies worked for you? Why? Which strategies didn't work for you? Why? Use your examples to support your answers.

Reading 1: The First Mile Under Four Minutes

Before You Read

Preview

A. The title of Reading 1 is "The First Mile Under Four Minutes." What do you think it's about? Discuss with a partner.

B. Take a *True/False* test to preview Reading 1. Circle *T* (True) or *F* (False) for each item. Guess at the answers you don't know.

1. The first person to run a mile in under four minutes was Roger Bannister.   T   F

2. He ran it before 1954.   T   F

3. He ran it in France.   T   F

4. Roger Bannister planned to study engineering.   T   F

5. Friends helped him train.   T   F

C. Compare your answers with a partner.

Vocabulary

Preview words and expressions from Reading 1. Complete the sentences below with a word or expression from the box.

ahead of	break the record	chased	crosswind
mechanics	no different from	track	training

1. All the boys on the team were about the same size. Jerry was _____

   _____ _____ the others.

2. Carl likes to run, so he decided to join the _____ team.

3. Susan wants to learn exactly what happens to the body when you run, so she is studying the

   _____ of running.

4. To prepare for the race, Jack ran two miles every morning and spent three hours in the gym

   every afternoon. This _____ helped him win the race.

5. In the last race, Carl ran very fast, but Jack ran faster. Jack won the race because he ran

   _____ _____ Carl.

6. Susan ran on the beach with her dog Skip. Skip saw another dog and ran after it. He

   _____ it into the water.

7. A wind behind you helps you run faster, but a wind from the side, a _____,
   slows you down.

8. Jack tried to do better than all the past runners. He tried to _____

   _____ _____ of the runners of the past.

As you read, think about this question:

▶ How was Roger Bannister different from other people?

🎧 The First Mile Under Four Minutes

People said that it couldn't be done. They said that no one could run a mile in less than four minutes. They said that it was impossible, and they gave good reasons. For example, they said that humans didn't have big enough lungs. They said that the human body was too big. They said that the human body was too heavy.

Then Roger Bannister came along. On May 6, 1954, he did it. He ran a mile in less than four minutes. How did he do it? Did he have big lungs? Was he smaller than other people? Was he lighter than other people? No, Bannister was no different from other people, except for one thing. Bannister believed in himself. He believed that with preparation he could break the four-minute mile.

Roger Bannister was born in Harrow, England, in 1929. At 17, he started college at Oxford University. He planned to study medicine. He was on the track team at Oxford, and he ran in races. He decided that it was possible to run a mile in less than four minutes. He used his medical knowledge to help him understand the human body, and he researched the mechanics of running. He developed a training program. He trained for thirty minutes every day during his lunch break.

Then Bannister tried to break the four-minute mile. He had a new idea about running. He knew that he ran fastest when chasing someone. Bannister asked two friends, Chris Chataway and Chris

Roger Bannister

Brasher, to help. On the day of the famous race, there was a big crowd. Chris Chataway ran very fast for the first half mile. Bannister chased him. Then Chris Brasher ran very fast for the second half mile. The friends were not racing against Bannister. They were helping him to run faster.

Bannister ran very fast. In the first half, Chris Chataway ran ahead of Bannister. It was hard to run because the crosswind was 15 miles per hour. Sometimes the wind got as strong as 25 miles per hour. After the first half mile, Bannister's time was 1:58.2. During the second half of the mile, his second friend, Chris Brasher, ran ahead of Bannister. At three-quarters of a mile, Bannister's time was 3:00.5. Bannister ran the last quarter-mile very fast. He ran ahead of Chris Brasher. When he finished running the mile, the announcer said, "Three ..." and the crowd started to shout. No one could hear the final time. It was three minutes, fifty-nine point four seconds. Roger Bannister did it. He was the first person to run a mile in less than four minutes.

Word Count: 435

Timed Reading

Read: "The First Mile Under Four Minutes" again. Read at a comfortable speed. Time your reading.

Start time: _____

End time: _____

My reading time: _____

After You Read

Comprehension

A. How was Roger Bannister different from other people? Fill in the bubble for the correct answer.

    (A) He had bigger lungs.

    (B) He believed in himself.

    (C) He was lighter.

B. Retake the *True/False* test you took on page 110. Change the false statements to make them true.

                Two
Example: ~~Three~~ friends helped Roger Bannister.   T   (F)

1. The first person to run a mile in under four minutes was Roger Bannister.   T   F

2. He ran it before 1954.   T   F

3. He ran it in France.   T   F

4. Roger Bannister planned to study engineering.   T   F

5. Friends helped him train.   T   F

Talk About It

Discuss the following questions:

1. Roger Bannister had his friends help him. Was that fair?

2. As of 2005, no woman has run a mile under four minutes. Do you think a woman will someday? Why or why not?

Was it fair Roger Bannister's friends helped him?

I think it . . .

Reading 2: Sports and History

Before You Read

Reading Skills

> ## Interacting with the Passage Before You Read
>
> You already know that good readers always interact with a reading passage. Before they read the passage completely, they scan (look over quickly) the major parts or sections of the passage. They also ask themselves questions about the title, headings, pictures, charts, diagrams, and captions. Then they try to answer their own questions. By asking questions about the important parts of a passage before you read, you interact with the information in the passage and remember it better.

Practice

Practice asking and answering your own pre-reading questions about "Sports and History" on pages 117–118. Scan the title, the headings, and anything else that you see. Write your questions and the answers on the following lines. If you are not sure of the answer, write *Not sure*.

1. Ask yourself a question about the reading title "Sports and History."

    Question: _____

    Answer: _____

2. Ask yourself a question about the first heading "Lacrosse: A Native American Sport."

    Question: _____

    Answer: _____

3. Ask yourself a question about the heading "Benjamin Franklin: Swimmer and Inventor."

    Question: _____

    Answer: _____

Preview

A. The title of Reading 2 is "Sports and History." What do you think it's about? Discuss with a partner.

B. On the left are some words about occupations from the reading. Match each one with the correct definition on the right. Write the letter of the definition next to the correct word.

_____ **1.** economist   **a.** a person who invents things

_____ **2.** inventor   **b.** an expert in science

_____ **3.** missionary   **c.** a person who prints books and newspapers

_____ **4.** musician   **d.** a person who thinks about ideas and philosophy

_____ **5.** philosopher   **e.** a person who studies the economy

_____ **6.** scientist   **f.** a person who does religious work

_____ **7.** printer   **g.** a person who plays music

As You Read

As you read, think about this question:
▶ What can the history of sports tell us?

🎧 Sports and History

Many sports that are popular today have a surprising history. Some sports were invented a long time ago. The history of sports can tell us about cross-cultural connections and imaginative inventions of the past.

Lacrosse: A Native American Sport

In the 1630s, a French missionary in New York described a game
5   that the Seneca Indians played. They played it with a stick. The missionary said that the stick looked like the "crosier," the stick that the bishop carried at religious ceremonies.

There were many myths about this game. Some people said that the game had no rules. Some said that every member of the tribe
10   played, so that there were 5,000 players on each team. Some said that players used human skulls, not balls. But none of this was true.

The game did have rules, but the rules could change. For example, the number of players on each team was either eight or twenty-two: eight players played on a small field while twenty-two played on
15   a large field. Sometimes four points was enough to win and some-

A bishop with a crosier

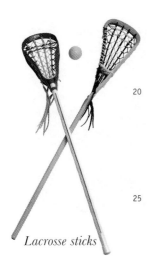

Lacrosse sticks

times seven points won. This was because four and seven were special numbers to the Seneca. (Most cultures have "lucky" numbers and "unlucky" numbers. For the Seneca Indians, both four and seven were lucky numbers.) The team captains agreed on the win-
20   ning number before the game began. Also, the balls were made of animal hair, not human skulls.

In the early 1800s, French pioneers started playing "lacrosse." The name of the game came from the playing sticks. In 1867, a Canadian dentist, W. George Beers, wrote down the rules of
25   lacrosse. Today, people play lacrosse at colleges and universities all over North America.

Chapter 6 Sports History ◆ 117

Benjamin Franklin

Benjamin Franklin: Swimmer and Sports Inventor

Benjamin Franklin (1706–1790) was a famous American. He did many things during his long life. He was a scientist, an inventor, a statesman, a printer, a philosopher, a musician, and an economist. He was also a swimmer. He swam in the ocean near Boston, Massachusetts. The water was extremely cold, so he designed and wore a wetsuit. The wetsuit kept him warm. People use wetsuits today. For example, scuba divers wear wetsuits to stay warm for a long time in very cold water.

One day, Franklin got an idea about a new sport from flying his kite. He was standing by a small lake. He thought that a person could hold one end of a rope tied to a really big kite. The kite could pull the person across the water. Franklin tried it and it worked. Today windsurfers use a big sail to pull themselves across the water. This works like Franklin's kite. People also use big kites to pull themselves across ice, snow, sand, and waves.

A modern wetsuit

Franklin had another idea: A person could put flat pieces of wood on their feet and go even faster in the water. This didn't work. The wood was too heavy. But Franklin drew the designs and wrote about his idea anyway. Today, people put rubber fins on their feet. The fins help them move faster in the water.

Word Count: 515

Timed Reading

Read "Sports and History" again. Read at a comfortable speed. Time your reading.

Start time: _____

End time: _____

My reading time: _____

Windsurfing

After You Read

Main Idea

What is the main idea of "Sports and History"? Fill in the bubble for the correct answer.

(A) The history of sports tells us that some sports are new and some are old.

(B) The history of sports tells us that in the past, sports did not have rules.

(C) The history of sports tells us about cross-cultural connections and inventions of the past.

Reading Skills

Predicting Questions for a Test

Teachers often test you on what you read. How do you know what to remember from a reading? The most important information in a passage is usually the main idea, the supporting ideas, and the details that support and explain the main and supporting ideas.

Example:

1. In Reading 2 you read, "The French learned about lacrosse from the Seneca Indians."

2. You ask yourself, "Is this important?"

3. You decide, "Yes, because it's an example of the main idea: Sports can tell us about cross-cultural connections."

4. You read, "There were 5,000 players on a team."

5. You ask yourself, "Is this important?"

6. You decide, "No, it's not true and it doesn't support or explain the main idea, so there's no reason to remember it."

Practice

Practice finding information in a passage that might be on a test.

A. Look at the following list of specific details from "Sports and History." Check (✓) the ones that might be on a test. Draw a line through the ones that probably won't be on a test. Compare your answers with a partner.

_____ 1. Some said lacrosse had no rules.

_____ 2. Some said human skulls were used.

_____ **3.** The rules of lacrosse could change.

_____ **4.** George Beers was a Canadian dentist.

_____ **5.** George Beers wrote down the rules of lacrosse.

_____ **6.** Benjamin Franklin lived a long life.

_____ **7.** Benjamin Franklin had the idea that led to rubber fins.

_____ **8.** Benjamin Franklin was standing by a lake when he got his idea about windsurfing.

B. Now find important information on your own. In Chapter 4, you learned to take notes on your reading. This time, take notes on important ideas in "Sports and History." Note the ideas that you think might be on a test. Look for the main idea, the supporting ideas, and the examples and details that explain the main and supporting ideas. Write your notes in the margins.

Getting the Details

In "Sports and History" some of the details about lacrosse are correct and some are incorrect. Some of the information about Benjamin Franklin is about his successes and some is about his failures. Answer the questions below.

1. How did the Seneca Indians play lacrosse? Find the correct information.

    a. number of players: _____

    b. number of winning points: _____

    c. balls were made of: _____

2. Were the following inventions successes or failures when Franklin invented them? Write _Success_ or _Failure_ next to each one.

    a. wetsuit: _____

    b. windsurfing sail: _____

    c. swimmer's fins: _____

Vocabulary

A. Here are some more words and expressions from "Sports and History." Find them in the reading passage and circle them.

Nouns	Adjectives	Adverb
myths	flat	extremely
rope	religious	
skulls		

B. Now use them to complete the sentences below.

1. Franklin used _____ pieces of wood on his feet instead of round pieces, because round pieces would not help him move in the water.

2. Human _____ are lighter than stones. They have a round shape so some scientists think they were used as balls.

3. Vince is a missionary and he believes in God. He is a _____ person.

4. Here is a very strong piece of cord to tie up the boat. Only a piece of

   _____ like this will be strong enough to keep it tied up.

5. There were many stories about lacrosse. Some were true, but some were

   _____.

6. It's very hard to become a good surfer. In fact, it is _____ hard.

Talk About It

Discuss the following questions:
1. Do you know the history of any other sports? If so, share your information.
2. List the sports you know. Which ones are the oldest? Which ones are newest?
3. What inventions do you use to help you play your favorite sport? Do they make you a better player? Do they keep you from getting hurt?

Do you know the history of any sports?

I know the history of . . .

Expressions

Talking about Age and Time

In English, time expressions are a combination of prepositions and written or numerical numbers:

at + age	At 17, Roger Bannister started college.
on + specific date	On May 6, 1954, he ran a four-minute mile.
in + period of time	In the 1630s, a French missionary in New York described a game that the Seneca Indians played.

Practice

A. Find and underline these expressions in "The First Mile Under Four Minutes" or "Sports and History."

at 17	in 1929	in the early 1800s
in the 1630s	In 1867	on May 6, 1954

B. Now use them to complete the sentences below.

1. Roger Bannister was born _____ _____.

2. Bannister entered Oxford University _____ _____.

3. He ran the mile in under four minutes for the first time _____

   _____ _____ _____.

4. A French missionary described the game with sticks that the Seneca Indians played

   _____ _____ _____.

5. French pioneers started playing lacrosse _____

   _____ _____ _____.

6. _____ _____ W. George Beers wrote down the rules of lacrosse.

Internet Research

Finding a Biography on the Internet

The Internet is a great place to find biographical information about famous people. Finding biographies is easy. Just go to a search engine such as Google (www.google.com). Type the name of the person into the text box with the word *biography* next to it.

Example:

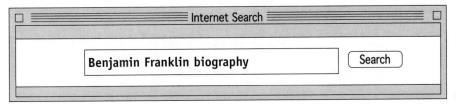

You can limit your search by putting quotes around the entire expression. Also, remember to look carefully at the URL—it tells you a lot about the source of the information. (Note: You don't have to use capitals in a search.)

You can also go to websites that specialize in biographies. An example is www.biography.com.

Practice

Find the biography of a famous athlete on the Internet. Print the best example and bring it to class. Discuss it with your classmates: What keywords did you use? Did you use quotes? Did the URL help you choose the best result? Did you use a search engine or a biography site?

Write About It

A. Write the following paragraphs. Fill in the blanks. Write complete sentences.

Paragraph One

There are two ways to improve at _____ .
[Give the name of a sport or an activity]

One way is _____ . This works
[Explain the strategy]

because _____ . Another way to
[Explain the reason as well as you can]

improve is _____ . This works because
[Explain the strategy]

_____ .
[Explain the reason as well as you can]

Paragraph Two

In my opinion, the best sports invention is _____ .
[Give an invention]

It is useful because _____
[Explain the reason as well as you can]

_____ . Another good sports invention is _____ .
[Give another invention]

This is useful because _____ .
[Explain the reason as well as you can]

B. Now write your own paragraphs. First, write one paragraph about ways to improve at a sport or an activity. Then write another about the best sports inventions. Try to include five new words or expressions from this chapter.

C. Write more paragraphs about sports and history. Here are some ideas:

▶ Write about the first time you played a sport.

▶ Answer these questions: What sport do you play? When did you start? What do you do to train? What do you do to improve?

▶ Describe the athlete that you found in your Internet search. Do not just copy what you find on the Internet. Make sure you use your own words.

▶ Your own idea

Include five new words or expressions from this chapter in your paragraphs. Also, try to use your Internet research.

On Your Own

Project

Design a survey. Ask your classmates about their sports history.

Step 1: Practice

With a partner, design a survey about sports history. Think of three questions. Write your questions in the survey box below. Have your teacher check them to make sure that they are correct. Repeat the questions with your teacher so you can pronounce them correctly.

Step 2: Take a Survey

Ask three classmates your questions below about their sports history. Indicate *M* (male) or *F* (female) for each person.

Sports History Survey

1. Question: _____

Person 1   M _____   F _____ Answer: _____

Person 2   M _____   F _____ Answer: _____

Person 3   M _____   F _____ Answer: _____

2. Question: _____

Person 1   Answer: _____

Person 2   Answer: _____

Person 3   Answer: _____

3. Question: _____

Person 1   Answer: _____

Person 2   Answer: _____

Person 3   Answer: _____

Step 3: Follow-Up

Explain the results of your survey to the class. For example, you could say, "I asked three people about their sports history. Two people said that they started playing soccer at age five. One said that she played on a team at school."

Wrap Up

How Much Do You Remember?

Check your new knowledge. In this chapter you learned facts, words, and expressions. You also learned reading skills and you practiced writing. Complete the following to check what you remember.

1. How did Roger Bannister's friends help him run a mile in under four minutes?

   _____

2. Which Native American tribe played lacrosse?

   _____

3. List three things that Benjamin Franklin invented.

   _____

4. Use *inventor* in a sentence.

   _____

5. Use *in* + (specific period of time) in a sentence.

   _____

6. How can you find a biography on the Internet?

   _____

Second Timed Readings

Now reread "The First Mile Under Four Minutes" and "Sports and History." Time each reading separately. Write your times for all the Timed Readings in this chapter in the Timed Reading Chart on page 214.

Crossword Puzzle

Complete the crossword puzzle to practice some words from this chapter.

CLUES

Across →

3. Wind from the side
6. The opposite of *round*
8. Stories that are not true are _____.

Down ↓

1. A strong cord
2. Pioneers started playing lacrosse _____ the early 1800s.
3. The dog _____ the cat.
4. Ben Franklin was a great _____.
5. Bones of human heads
7. He went to the university _____ 17.

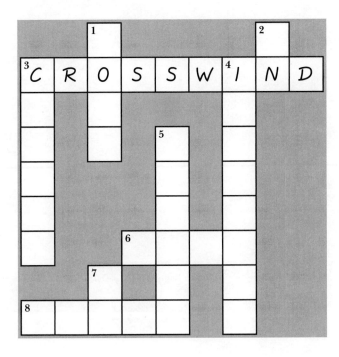

What is Biology?

Biology is one of the life sciences. It's the study of living things and their environments. Biologists study plants, animals, and humans. Biologists also improve food crops, develop medicines, and work with animals and their habitats. Biology has many areas. Some of them are

- plant biology
- marine biology
- ecology
- genetics
- biochemistry
- cell biology
- microbiology

The ancient Egyptians, Babylonians, and Greeks left records of their work in biology. For example, the Greek philosopher Aristotle (384–322 B.C.) studied medicine and classified and described many life forms including bees, chickens, whales, dolphins, sharks, and octopuses.

SOME FAMOUS BIOLOGISTS

Some of the scientists who made important discoveries in biology include:

Antony van Leeuwenhoek—The Netherlands, 1632–1723
Invented the microscope

Carl Linnaeus—Sweden, 1707–1778
Developed a classification system for living things

Charles Darwin—English, 1809–1882
Developed the theory of evolution

Gregor Mendel—Austria, 1822–1884
Described heredity

Francis Harry Compton Crick—English, 1916–
With J.D. Watson, described the structure of DNA

Barbara McClintock—American, 1902–1992
Won the Nobel Prize for her work in genetics

Biology and You

Biologists can teach at universities or do research for government agencies, pharmaceutical companies, or hospitals. Biologists also sell chemicals, drugs, or laboratory instruments, and write for technical publications.

Do you want to study biology? Ask yourself these questions:

- Am I interested in plants, animals, and people?
- Am I good at observing and describing?
- Do I enjoy doing experiments?
- Am I careful and patient?
- Am I a creative thinker?
- Do I like math and science?

CHAPTER 7

Nature or Nurture

CHAPTER PREVIEW

In this chapter, you'll:

Content
▶ read about identical twins
▶ read about the debate on nature vs. nurture

Reading Skills
▶ use the introductory paragraph to preview a reading
▶ identify facts and opinions

Vocabulary Skills
▶ use words and expressions to talk about nature and nurture
▶ use words and expressions to talk about characteristics

Writing Skills
▶ write about nature and nurture

Research Skills
▶ find recent news on the Internet
▶ interview people about their opinions of the nature vs. nurture debate

SHORT SURVEY

Who in your family do you look the most like?

❑ my mother

❑ my father

❑ my grandmother

❑ my grandfather

❑ another relative: _____

Reading 1:

What happens to twins separated at birth? Read "Twins: Separated at Birth" to find out.

Reading 2:

Which is more important, nature or nurture? Read "Nature *and* Nurture" to find out.

What do you think?

Look at the following characteristics. Did you *inherit* them (have at them at birth) or did you learn them? Decide and check (✓) the correct box, "Inherited" or "Learned."

	Inherited	Learned
Weight		
Height		
Intelligence (how smart you are)		
Your ability to make friends		
Sense of humor		
Ability to spell correctly		
The kind of food that you like to eat		
The sports that you like to play		
The sound of your voice		

Compare your answers with a partner. Then discuss the following questions:

1. Do you have brothers or sisters? If yes, how are you the same? How are you different?
2. In your opinion, is personality (for example, being shy) learned or inherited?

Do you have brothers or sisters?

I have. . .

Reading 1: Twins: Separated at Birth

Before You Read

Preview

A. The title of Reading 1 is "Twins: Separated at Birth." What do you think it's about? Discuss with a partner.

B. Take the following quiz. Guess if you aren't sure. Fill in the bubble for each correct answer.

1. How many kinds of twins are there?
   - Ⓐ There are three kinds of twins.
   - Ⓑ There are two kinds of twins.
   - Ⓒ There is one kind of twin.

2. Which is true about fraternal twins?
   - Ⓐ They develop from two eggs.
   - Ⓑ Their fathers are fraternal twins.
   - Ⓒ They are always brothers.

3. What is true about identical twins?
   - Ⓐ They develop from one egg.
   - Ⓑ Their mothers are identical twins.
   - Ⓒ They are sister and brother.

4. What can happen if identical twins are separated at birth?
   - Ⓐ They usually never see each other again.
   - Ⓑ They often become very different people.
   - Ⓒ They often have many similarities in their lives.

5. Why do scientists study twins separated at birth?
   - Ⓐ Twins separated at birth are very common and easy to find.
   - Ⓑ Twins separated at birth help to answer the question, "Which is more important, nature or nurture?"
   - Ⓒ Twins separated at birth have emotional problems.

Vocabulary

Preview the words from Reading 1 on the left. Match them with their definitions on the right. Write the letter of the definition next to the correct word.

Identical twins

Fraternal twins

Siblings

1. _____ adopt

2. _____ candidates

3. _____ DNA

4. _____ fraternal twins

5. _____ identical twins

6. _____ reunited

7. _____ siblings

a. twins coming from two eggs

b. came together again

c. brothers and sisters

d. twins coming from one egg

e. raise a child who is not your biological child

f. acids that are the basis of heredity

g. people who want to be elected to a political position

As you read, think about this question:

▶ Were the twins Theo and Jim alike or different after they grew up?

🎧 Twins: Separated at Birth

One out of every 70 births is twins. There are two kinds of twins, fraternal and identical. Fraternal twins develop from two eggs.
5 They are like any other siblings (sisters and brothers), but they are the same age. They may look alike, and they may not. They may have the same likes and dislikes, but they
10 may not. Sometimes people can tell that the two siblings are twins, but

sometimes they can't. Fraternal twins can be two boys, two girls, or a boy and a girl. One third of all twins are identical. Identical twins develop from one egg. They share the same DNA. They are very much alike in the way that they
15 look, talk, and act. They can only be two boys or two girls. People often have a hard time telling identical twins apart. They look the same to most people. Besides looking alike, identical twins often share the same hopes, dreams, and goals. Scientists also find that they share the same taste in food and the same eating habits. For example, identical twins often feel full after eating the same
20 amount of food.

Identical twins are alike in many ways. Theo Jones and Jim Tomas are an example. They are identical twins. However, Theo and Jim were separated early in life—different families adopted them soon after they were born. Thirty-nine years later, they reunited. They were surprised by the many similarities in their lives.

Here are some of the similarities that the twins discovered when they met again: Both Theo and Jim married two times. Each married a woman named Susan the first time. Each married a woman named Nadia the second time. They both had dogs named Roy. They both smoked, liked beer, and drove big cars. Theo and Jim had other surprising similarities, too. They both chewed their fingernails. They both voted for the same candidates in the last three elections. And they both loved their second wives and left love notes around the house.

Scientists like to study twins. Twins who are separated at birth help them answer the question: Which is more important, nature or nurture?

Word Count: 359

Timed Reading

Read "Twins: Separated at Birth" again. Read at a comfortable speed. Time your reading.

Start time: _____

End time: _____

My reading time: _____

After You Read

Comprehension

Fill in the bubble for each correct answer.

1. How many types of twins are there?

   (A) one type   (B) two types   (C) three types

2. What is *not* similar about Theo and Jim?

   (A) their looks   (B) their hopes   (C) their names

3. What happened to Theo and Jim early in life?

   (A) Doctors studied their DNA.   (B) They were adopted.   (C) They dressed alike.

4. What is not true about Theo and Jim?

   (A) They voted for the same candidates in the last three elections.

   (B) They left love notes around the house for their wives.

   (C) One had a dog name Boy and the other had a dog named Roy.

5. Which question do scientists try to answer when they study twins separated at birth?

   (A) Which is more important, dreams or goals?

   (B) Do twins separated at birth have emotional problems?

   (C) Which is more important, nature or nurture?

Talk About It

Discuss the following questions:

1. Are you a twin? If yes, do you like being a twin? Why or why not? If no, would you like to be a twin? Why or why not? What are the advantages and disadvantages of being a twin?

2. What do you think about the study of twins? Does it help other people or does it only help twins?

Are you a twin?

Yes, I am.

Reading 2: Nature and Nurture

Before You Read

Preview

A. The title of Reading 2 is "Nature *and* Nurture." What do you think it's about? Discuss with a partner.

B. Preview the following words from Reading 2. Complete each of the sentences below with the correct word.

> appearance   debate   environment
> genes   overcomes   versus

1. Albert thinks he will live a long time because his mother and father lived to be 90. He

   believes he has good _____.

2. When people say "nature or nurture," they sometimes replace *or* with the Latin word for

   against. They say, "nature _____ nurture."

3. There are two sides of the nature and nurture issue. In fact, this _____ is
   very old. People have been discussing it for hundreds of years.

4. "I grew up in a good home. My adopted parents were kind and helpful. I was lucky to live in

   such a nice _____," said Sarah.

5. Some people say that the way you look is inherited. But I think that your lifestyle affects

   your _____. For example, too much sun can make you look old at an
   early age.

6. Some people think that nurture is more important than nature. In fact, studies on

   intelligence show that nurture _____ nature.

Reading Skills

Practice

A. Read just the introduction to "Nature *and* Nurture" on pages 139–140. Locate and write down the main idea, definitions, and information about how the passage is organized.

Main idea: _____

_____

Definitions: _____

_____

Organization: _____

_____

B. Now discuss your answers with a partner.

As you read, think about this question:
▶ Do intelligence and appearance come from heredity (nature) or environment (nurture)?

> It's not where you come from, it's where you go. ?❧
>
> —*Joel Siegel,*
> *(American journalist, b. 1946)*

🎧 Nature *and* Nurture

For centuries, people have wondered which is more important: *nature* or *nurture*. Nature means heredity—what you get at birth from your parents, such as your eye color and hair color. Nurture means everything else in your life— what happens after you are born, such as where you live and what you eat. The
5 question is a difficult one: Are we born with our looks and intelligence? Do looks and intelligence develop after we are born?

A Short History

In the late 19th century, Francis Galton, a British scientist, invented the famous expression "nature *versus* nurture." At times throughout history, people thought nature was more important. At other times, they thought nurture was more impor-
10 tant. In the beginning of the 20th century, most people believed that nature was more important. Later, in the 1940s and 1950s, people believed that nurture was more important. In 1979, researchers in Minnesota began a major study of identical twins who lived apart. This study showed the importance of nature. More recent-ly, however, some research is showing that nurture is more important.

15 The debate continues. But most scientists agree that both nature and nurture are important. Intelligence and appearance are two examples of how nature and nurture work together.

Intelligence

Most scientists think that intelligence is a combination of heredity and envi-ronment. We are born with a potential (possibility) for intelligence. Our genes
20 determine this. However, events after birth are important, too. For example, edu-cation and good nutrition can improve intelligence. There are many ways of defin-ing intelligence. One way is the IQ (Intelligence Quotient) test. Research shows that a positive environment can lead to higher scores on standardized IQ tests.

For example, some people who study babies and children think that the way
25 parents talk to their children can improve IQ. A study at the Speech, Language

and Hearing Centre in London showed this. They studied 140 nine-month-old babies. They taught half of the parents how to talk to their babies. The other half of the parents had no training. After seven years, they tested the children. Nine of the children in the group with specially trained parents had IQs of more than
30   130. None of the children in the other group had such high IQs.

Appearance

Appearance is also a combination of genes and environment. Do genes affect the way we look as we get older? Or does environment? A New York plastic surgeon, Darrick E. Antell, MD, wondered about
35   this. He studied two twins, Gay and Gwyn. When they were children, people couldn't tell Gay and Gwyn apart. But today, even though Gay and Gwyn

Gwyn   *Gay*

are genetically identical, they look quite different. Gay looks much older than Gwyn. Gay has deep lines in her face. Gwyn's skin is smooth.

40   Dr. Antell learned about their history. Both were divorced. Both had children. They had the same job. Gay lived in California and spent a lot of time in the sun. She smoked a pack of cigarettes a day. Gwyn, on the other hand, lived in Maryland, and she spent less time in the sun. She never smoked. Dr. Antell thinks that sun and smoking caused Gay to look much older than her twin.

Balancing Nature and Nurture

45   People continue to discuss nature and nurture. In the seventeenth century, the writer James Howell said, "Nurture overcomes nature." In the twenty-first century, Matt Ridley, a science writer, says, "Nature versus nurture is dead. Long live nature via (through) nurture." What do you think?

Word Count: 593

Timed Reading

Read "Nature *and* Nurture" again. Read at a comfortable speed. Time your reading.

Start time: _____

End time: _____

My reading time: _____

After You Read

Main Idea

What is the main idea of "Nature *and* Nurture"? Fill in the bubble for the correct answer.

- (A) Nature and nurture are both important.
- (B) Intelligence and appearance are equally important.
- (C) Most people think nurture is more important than nature.

Getting the Details

Answer the following questions. Fill in the bubble for each correct answer.

1. Who invented the expression *nature versus nurture*?

   (A) Francis Galton   (B) Darrick E. Antell, MD   (C) James Howell

2. What does IQ tell about people?

   - (A) how much their parents talked to them
   - (B) how much time they spend in the library
   - (C) how intelligent they are

3. What did the study at the Speech, Language and Hearing Centre in London show?

   - (A) Parents do not need training to talk to children.
   - (B) Training parents does not help their children.
   - (C) Parents can help increase their children's IQ.

4. When they were children, people _____.

   - (A) thought Gay was older than Gwyn
   - (B) couldn't tell Gay and Gwyn apart
   - (C) thought that Gwyn looked different from Gay

5. What is *not* true of Gay and Gwyn?

   (A) Both smoked.   (B) Both were divorced.   (C) Both had children.

Reading Skills

Identifying Facts and Opinions

When you read, it's important to know the difference between fact and opinion. A fact is an idea that has evidence. It can be proved. An opinion cannot be proved.

Read this sentence: "Francis Galton, a British scientist, invented the famous expression 'nature versus nurture.'"

Does it express a fact? Yes. You know because you can look Galton up in a book and find that he is a British scientist and that he was the first one to use the expression "nature vs. nurture."

Now read this sentence: "Most scientists think that intelligence is a combination of heredity and environment."

Does it express a fact? No. It tells the opinion of "most scientists." Do we really know what most scientists think? No, we cannot prove what most scientists think. The writer is telling us what he thinks. This is the writer's opinion. Opinion statements often include words such as *think, believe,* and *feel.*

Practice

Read each of the following statements. Decide if it expresses a fact or an opinion. Check (✓) the correct box.

	Fact	Opinion
1. In 1979, researchers in Minnesota began a major study of identical twins.		
2. IQ means Intelligence Quotient.		
3. The Hearing Centre studied 140 babies.		
4. Some people who study babies and children think that the way parents talk to their children can improve IQ.		
5. Dr. Antell thinks that sun and smoking caused Gay to look much older than her twin.		

Vocabulary

A. Here are some more words from "Nature *and* Nurture." Find them in the passage and circle them.

Nouns	Adjective	Verb
heredity IQ training	standardized	affect

B. Now use the words to complete the sentences below.

1. Yolanda took an intelligence test. Her _____ was 120. It showed that she was a very intelligent child. A child of average intelligence has a score of 100.

2. Certain characteristics are a result of _____. You are born with your eye color—your environment cannot change that characteristic.

3. Parents want their children to be intelligent, so they sometimes get _____ from professional teachers to learn how to improve their children's intelligence.

4. Studies show that nutrition can _____ intelligence. This means a child's lifestyle can make her more or less intelligent.

5. Examples of _____ tests are the TOEFL and the SAT. Those tests are carefully designed to get accurate results.

Talk About It

Discuss the following questions:
1. Which do you think is more important, *nature* or *nurture*?
2. Imagine you have money to study twins. What is your research plan? Will you study personality, appearance, intelligence, habits, or something else?

Which do you think is more important?

I think . . .

Expressions

> ## Talking about Nature and Nurture
>
> Here are some expressions for talking about *nature* and *nurture*:
>
> (be) born with   a combination of heredity and environment   develop after
> develop from   (be) separated at birth   share the same DNA
>
> Example:
> Jim and Theo <u>were separated at birth</u>.

Practice

A. Find and underline these expressions in "Twins: Separated at Birth" or "Nature *and* Nurture."

B. Now use them to complete the following sentences.

1. From birth, Sam was happy, easygoing, and cheerful. He was _____

   _____ these qualities.

2. No one knew that Rob would be a great tennis player. We saw these abilities

   _____ _____ he was a child.

3. Dan was excited to find his twin brother. They grew up separately. In fact, he and his twin

   were _____ _____ _____.

4. Identical twins have the same genes. They _____

   _____ _____ _____.

5. Susan's babies will be identical twins if they _____

   _____ one egg.

6. Most scientists believe that both nature and nurture are important. They think that

   _____ _____ _____

   _____ _____ _____

   makes us who we are.

Internet Research

Finding News on the Internet

Many websites have the latest news. Examples include Google and Yahoo. They are a great way to find up-to-date information about a topic that you are interested in.

To get news, go to a website that has news such as Google (www.google.com). Look for the "News" section and click on it. When you get to the news page, type the topic that you want into the text box.

Example:

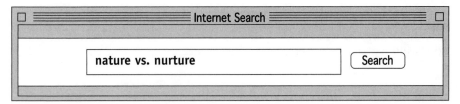

Note that the date and the name of the newspaper will appear in the results. This can help you choose the best source. Remember, you can limit your search by putting quotes around the entire expression. Also, you don't have to use capitals in a search.

Practice

Look for news about *twins, twins separated at birth, nature and nurture, nature vs. nurture, heredity,* or *environment* on a news website. Print the best news story and bring it to class.

With a partner discuss the following questions:
- ▶ What keywords did you use?
- ▶ Did you use quotes?
- ▶ How many results did you get?
- ▶ Which newspapers had results?
- ▶ On what date were the stories published?

Write About It

A. Write the following paragraphs. Fill in the blanks. Write complete sentences.

Paragraph One

I believe that nature/nurture _____ is more important
        [Circle one]   [Write your choice]

for two reasons. The first reason is that _____
                           [Explain the reason]

_____.
             [Explain the reason]

The second reason is that _____
                  [Explain the reason]

_____.

Paragraph Two

I am a combination of my heredity and my environment. Because of my heredity, I

_____
   [Discuss characteristics that you inherited, such as appearance, personality, intelligence, or abilities]

_____.

At the same time, my environment is also important. Because of my environment, I

_____
   [Discuss how your environment affects your home, school, nutrition, or habits]

_____.

B. Now write your own paragraphs about nature and nurture. Try to include five new words or expressions from this chapter in your paragraph.

C. Write more paragraphs about nature and nurture. Here are some ideas:
- ▶ Write about the advantages or disadvantages of being a twin.
- ▶ Write about the news story that you found on the Internet.
- ▶ Give your opinion: Which is more important, research on heredity or research on environment? Why?

On Your Own

Project

Take a survey. Ask your classmates about their opinions on nature and nurture.

Step 1: Practice

Practice saying the questions in the survey box below. Repeat the questions with your teacher so you can pronounce them correctly.

Nature vs. Nurture Survey

1. In your opinion, what is more important, nature or nurture? Why?

   Person 1 _____ M _____ F   Answer: _____

   _____

   Person 2 _____ M _____ F   Answer: _____

   _____

   Person 3 _____ M _____ F   Answer: _____

   _____

2. In your opinion, is appearance more a result of heredity or environment? Explain.

   Person 1   Answer: _____

   Person 2   Answer: _____

   Person 3   Answer: _____

3. In your opinion, is intelligence more a result of heredity or environment? Explain.

   Person 1   Answer: _____

   Person 2   Answer: _____

   Person 3   Answer: _____

Step 2: Take a Survey

Ask three classmates the questions about nature and nurture.

Step 3: Follow Up

Explain the results of your survey to the class.

Wrap Up

How Much Do You Remember?

Check your new knowledge. In this chapter you learned facts, words, and expressions. You also learned reading skills and you practiced writing. Complete the following to check what you remember.

1. What are identical twins?

   _____

2. What did the Minnesota study of identical twins show?

   _____

3. Use the expression *develop from* in a sentence.

   _____

4. Give an example of a fact.

   _____

5. Give an example of an opinion.

   _____

6. How can you find recent news stories on the Internet?

   _____

Second Timed Readings

Now reread "Twins: Separated at Birth" and "Nature *and* Nurture." Time each reading separately. Write your times for all the Timed readings in this chapter in the Timed Reading Chart on page 215.

Crossword Puzzle

Complete the crossword puzzle to practice some words or expressions from this chapter.

CLUES

Across →
1. The basis of heredity
5. Against
8. Two children from one egg
9. Intelligence Quotient

Down ↓
2. Looks
3. What you get at birth from your parents
4. A person who wants to be elected
6. Brothers or sisters
7. Are we _____ _____ with our looks and intelligence or are they the results of environment?

CHAPTER 8

Oddities in Living Nature

CHAPTER PREVIEW

In this chapter, you'll:

Content
▶ find out about the relationship between size and lifespan in animals

▶ discover how some unusual animals survive in extreme environments

Reading Skills
▶ use topic sentences to preview a reading

▶ use context clues to guess the meanings of unknown words

Vocabulary Skills
▶ use words that describe size and lifespan in animals

▶ use words that describe extreme environments

▶ use words that describe animal behavior

Writing Skills
▶ write about animals, longevity, and adaptation

Research Skills
▶ use an online science dictionary

▶ get information on an animal that lives in an extreme environment

Animals are such agreeable friends; they ask no questions, pass no criticisms. ❧

—George Eliot
(British author, 1819–1880)

SHORT SURVEY

Where is the most difficult place to live on earth?

❑ the desert

❑ the South Pole

❑ the rain forest

❑ at high altitude (for example, on a mountain top)

❑ other _____

Reading 1:
Does an elephant live longer than a human? Read "Size and Life Span" to find out.

Reading 2:
What animal lives for over 200 years at the bottom of the ocean? Read about extreme environments to find out.

Take the following longevity (long life) quiz. Compare your answers with a partner.

Longevity Quiz

How long will you live? What contributes to a long life? Take this quiz.

My age: _____

My gender: ___ M   ___ F

My blood pressure:
___ Don't know   ___ Normal   ___ High

Height: _____   **Weight:** _____

Number of family members with heart disease before age 55:
___ None   ___ One   ___ Two or more

Exercise:
___ Daily   ___ A few times a week   ___ Once a week   ___ Occasionally   ___ Never

Stress:
___ I live in a very stressful environment.   ___ I live in a somewhat stressful environment.
___ I never feel stress.

Driving: ___ I use a seatbelt.   ___ I do not use a seatbelt.

Smoking:
___ I have never smoked.   ___ I quit more than two years ago.   ___ I quit less than two years ago.
___ I smoke less than one pack a day.   ___ I smoke more than one pack a day.

Diet:
___ I have an average diet.   ___ I eat a lot of junk food.
___ I eat five or more servings of fruit and vegetables a day.

We can't really tell you how long you will live. However, females live longer than males. Also, the following leads to longevity: no history of heart disease, regular exercise, having a low-stress environment, driving carefully and using seatbelts, not smoking, and eating a lot of fruits and vegetables. How long will *you* live?

Now discuss with a partner your answers to these questions:
1. How long do you think you'll live? Why?
2. What else contributes to long life?
3. What do you know about longevity in other animals? For example, which animal do you think lives the longest?

Reading 1: Size and Life Span

Before You Read

Preview

A. The title of Reading 1 is "Size and Life Span." What do you think it's about? Discuss with a partner.

B. Take the following quiz. Guess if you aren't sure. Fill in the bubble for each correct answer.

Blue whale

African elephants

Horse

1. Which animal lives the longest?

   Ⓐ blue whale   Ⓑ African elephant   Ⓒ horse

2. Which animal weighs the most?

   Ⓐ blue whale   Ⓑ African elephant   Ⓒ horse

3. Which animal has the slowest heart rate?

   Ⓐ blue whale   Ⓑ African elephant   Ⓒ horse

Vocabulary

Match the words from Reading 1 on the left with their definitions on the right. Write the correct letter of the definition next to the correct word. Work in small groups.

_____ 1. approximate   **a.** about; not exact

_____ 2. (be) an exception   **b.** speed

_____ 3. life span   **c.** the speed at which a living thing uses energy

_____ 4. mammals   **d.** warm-blooded animals that have live births

_____ 5. metabolism   **e.** the time of being alive

_____ 6. organism   **f.** a living thing

_____ 7. rate   **g.** excluded; not like the rest

_____ 8. species   **h.** a class or group of living things

As you read, think about this question:

► Which animals live longer, small ones or large ones?

> Nature's greatest
> masterpiece, an Elephant,
> the only harmless great
> thing; the giant of beast. 🐌
>
> —*John Donne*
> *(English poet, 1572–1631)*

🎧 Size and Life Span

Some biologists are interested in how long different types of animals live. They are particularly interested in why one type of animal lives a long time and another type of animal lives only a short time. Studies show that life span is related to metabolism. Metabolism is the rate at which an organism (a living thing) uses energy. With mammals, the larger the animal, the longer it lives. This is because larger mammals have slower metabolisms. This is generally true, although because of modern medicine, humans are an exception.

Mammals with slower metabolisms burn energy more slowly and have slower heart rates. For example, an elephant, the largest land mammal, has a heart rate of about 30 beats per minute. An elephant lives a relatively long life of about 70 years. The tiny shrew, on the other hand, has a heart rate of about 600 beats per minute. A shrew has a life span of about one and a half years.

Elephants

Shrew

The following table indicates the size, heart rate, and lifespan of various animals:

Animal	Height/Weight	Heart Rate/bpm	Life Span/Years
Shrew (American)	6 inches (15 cm) long; 0.4 ounces (11 gm)	600	1.5
Hamster	6–7 inches (15–18 cm) long; 0.4 ounces (13 gm)	330	2
Arctic seal	4 feet (1.2 m) long; 175 pounds (79 kg)	70	20
Polar bear	8–9 feet (2.4–2.7 m) long; 1,000 pounds (454 kg)	46	25
Lion	9 feet (2.7 m) long; 250–300 pounds (113–136 kg)	40	29
Horse	5 feet (1.5 m) tall; 1,300 pounds (590 kg)	45	25
African elephant	13 feet (4 m) tall; 7 tons (6.3 tonnes)	30	70
Human	5 feet, 10 inches (1.6 m) tall; 170 pounds (77 kg)	70	75
Blue whale	120 feet (36.6 m) long; 100 tons (91 tonnes)	20	200

bpm = beats per minute
Note: All amounts represent the average male of the species and are approximate.

For now, scientists are not certain why this relationship between metabolism and life span is true, but they hope to know soon.

Word Count: approx. 298

Timed Reading

Read "Size and Life Span" again. Read at a comfortable speed. Time your reading.

Start time: _____

End time: _____

My reading time: _____

After You Read

Comprehension

A. Which animals live longer, small ones or large ones?

B. Fill in the bubble for each correct answer.

1. Which statement is true?

   (A) Large mammals have faster heart rates than small animals.

   (B) Small mammals have slower metabolisms than large animals.

   (C) Metabolism is related to life span in all mammals.

2. Which of the following animals has a heart rate similar to the human heart rate?

   (A) horse   (B) Arctic seal   (C) polar bear

3. Which of the following animals has the fastest heart rate?

   (A) polar bear   (B) hamster   (C) shrew

4. Which of the following animals has the slowest heart rate?

   (A) lion   (B) African elephant   (C) horse

5. Which statement about the chart on page 155 is true?

   (A) The information describes any member of the species.

   (B) The information describes only the female of the species.

   (C) The information applies only to the male of the species.

Talk About It

Discuss the following questions:
1. When was the last time you went to the zoo? Which animals do you like to see?
2. What is your opinion of zoos? Is it O.K. to keep animals in cages for humans to see? Why or why not?

Reading 2: Extreme Environments

Before You Read

Preview

A. The title of Reading 2 is "Extreme Environments." What do you think it's about? Discuss with a partner.

B. Preview these words from the reading. Use them to complete the sentences below.

> adaptation   Carbon dioxide   flexible   hypothesis
> multi-celled   Oxygen   Ultraviolet light   vacuum

1. David looked at an organism under a microscope and noticed that it had many cells.

   However, he didn't know the name of this _____ organism.

2. _____ is a colorless, odorless gas. People need to breathe this gas to stay alive. If you are sick in the hospital, they may give you this gas.

3. _____ _____ is also a colorless, odorless gas. It is bad for people to breath, but plants use it to stay green.

4. This organism is very _____; it can live anywhere—in water, on land, and at high altitudes.

5. _____ _____ is a short wavelength light. It is invisible and can harm organisms. For example, if you sit outside on a sunny day, it will burn your skin.

6. Space with nothing in it is called a _____.

7. _____ is when animals change appearance and behavior in order to live in a particular environment. For example, polar bears have white fur because they live in the snow.

8. David had a _____ about the organism; he guessed that it could live both in and out of water.

Reading Skills

Using Topic Sentences to Preview a Reading Passage

In previous chapters, you used titles, headings, pictures, and captions to preview a reading passage. Another way to preview is to read topic sentences. Topic sentences tell you what the body (middle) paragraphs of a passage are about. Body paragraphs usually include supporting ideas and specific details. They support and explain the main idea of the entire passage. If you read the topic sentences, you can get a pretty good idea of how the author will support and explain his or her ideas. (Note: Topic sentences are often—but not always—the first sentence in each paragraph.)

Practice

A. Preview "Extreme Environments" on pages 159–160. Read and underline the first sentence of Paragraphs 3, 4, 5 and 6. Then write what you think each paragraph is about. Write your opinion on the following lines:

Paragraph 3: _____

_____

_____

Paragraph 4: _____

_____

_____

Paragraph 5: _____

_____

_____

Paragraph 6: _____

_____

_____

B. Now guess the main idea and predict some supporting ideas and details for "Extreme Environments." Share your predictions with a partner.

As you read, think about these questions:

▶ What are tubeworms and tardigrades? Why are they so unusual?

🎧 Extreme Environments

Organisms live in many environments, or habitats. The appearance and behavior of these organisms help them to survive in their habitats. This is called adaptation. Seals, for example, are designed for life in the sea. They store oxygen in their blood and in their muscles. This helps them hold their breath underwater for a long time. In addition, their bodies are designed to help them move quickly through the water. Other examples of adaptation include such things as the shape of a bird's beak and the color and thickness of an animal's fur.

There are thousands of interesting examples of animal adaptation. Some of the most unusual are animals that live in extreme environments. Extreme environments are places where it seems difficult to live. Examples include places that have little oxygen; places that are toxic (poisonous); or places that are very cold, very hot, or very dry.

Tubeworms Don't Eat

Tubeworms are an example of adaptation to an extreme environment. Tubeworms live 1,700 feet (518 kilometers) below the surface of the ocean. Not only do they survive at the bottom of the ocean, but tubeworms also live for up to 250 years, and they grow to over 10 feet (3.5 meters) long. Another amazing thing is that tubeworms don't eat. Instead, they get energy from toxic chemicals. These chemicals, such as sulphur, come out of cracks in the ocean floor.

Tubeworm

Scientists think that tubeworms are probably the longest living invertebrates. (Invertebrates are animals without backbones. Tortoises are the longest living vertebrates—animals with backbones.) But scientists aren't sure why tubeworms live so long. One hypothesis is that they live in a stress-free environment; that is, they live far from any other creatures that might bother them.

Tardigrades Can Live Anywhere

Tardigrade

The most interesting example of an organism that can live in an extreme environment is the tardigrade. Tardigrades are tiny, multi-celled organisms about 0.3 to 0.5 millimeters in size. That's about the size of the period at the end of this sentence. Tardigrades, also 30 known as "Water Bears" and "Moss Piglets," have five body segments and four pairs of short legs with claws on the end. They are aquatic (they need water to live), but they can live anywhere where there is water; they can live in fresh water, salt water, at high altitudes, in rain forests, and in deserts.

Tardigrades are very flexible creatures. They can live no matter what happens 35 to their environment. They survive in times of flood, drought, and even when there is no oxygen. For example, when there isn't enough oxygen, they blow up like a balloon and float around until they reach an atmosphere that has enough oxygen. When their environment gets too dry, they become smaller and go into a state called cryptobiosis. In this state, their metabolism stops. In fact, some 40 tardigrades have lived for over 100 years by going in and out of cryptobiosis. Scientists have tested tardigrades in laboratory experiments. Tests show that tardigrades can live in temperatures as low as $-457.6°F$ ($-272°C$) and in vacuums. The amazing tardigrade can also survive in carbon dioxide, ultraviolet light, and X-rays.

Word Count: 524

Timed Reading

Read "Extreme Enviroments" again. Read at a comfortable speed. Time your reading.

Start time: _____

End time: _____

My reading time: _____

After You Read

Main Idea

A. What is the main idea of "Extreme Environments"? Fill in the bubble for the correct answer.

Ⓐ Tubeworms are the longest living invertebrates.

Ⓑ Tardigrades can live anywhere.

Ⓒ Tardigrades and tubeworms are two examples of organisms that live in extreme environments.

B. Look at your preview predictions from page 158. Were you correct?

Getting the Details

A. Answer the following questions. Fill in the bubble for each correct answer.

1. Tubeworms may live so long because of their _____ environment.

Ⓐ chemical-free   Ⓑ toxic-free   Ⓒ stress-free

2. Tardigrades can live _____.

Ⓐ only in fresh water   Ⓑ anywhere   Ⓒ any place that has water

3. Tardigrades are very flexible. Another word for *flexible* is _____.

Ⓐ multi-celled   Ⓑ adaptable   Ⓒ tiny

4. Tardigrades can probably survive _____.

Ⓐ in the Arctic   Ⓑ in space   Ⓒ both A and B

B. Compare the tubeworm and the tardigrade. Compare their sizes, life spans, environments, and something that they need to survive. Work with a partner and use the chart.

	Size	Lifespan	Environment	Need to Live
Tubeworm				
Tardigrade				

Reading Skills

Guessing Meaning from Context Using a Given Definition

You can often guess the meaning of a new word by looking at its context (the words around it). There are many ways to guess using context. One way is to look for a definition nearby. Authors sometimes give definitions of new words. These definitions often follow certain types of punctuation such as parentheses ( ) and dashes (—). They also sometimes follow verbs such as *is/are* and *means*. These are context clues.

Examples:

Tardigrades sometimes go into cryptobiosis—a state in which their metabolism stops.
       New word   Definition

Adaptation is changing appearance and behavior in order to survive in a particular habitat.
New word   Definition

Practice

Find and underline the following words and expressions in Reading 2. Then look at the context of the word or phrase for a definition. Write each definition on the line and indicate the type of context clue that you found: ( ) (parentheses), — (dash), *is/are*, or *means*.

1. **Extreme environments:** _____

    Type of contextual clue: _____

2. **Toxic:** _____

    Type of contextual clue: _____

3. **Invertebrates:** _____

    Type of contextual clue: _____

4. **Vertebrates:** _____

    Type of contextual clue: _____

5. **Aquatic:** _____

    Type of contextual clue: _____

Vocabulary

A. Here are some words from "Extreme Environments." Find them in the passage and circle them.

Nouns	Verbs	Expression
altitudes drought Piglet segments	store survive	hold their breath

B. Now use them to complete the sentences below.

1. The tardigrade has five body parts. These _____ are very tiny; you need a microscope to see them.

2. Seals don't breath underwater; instead they _____

   _____ _____.

3. Certain types of plants _____ in the desert. They live well in very dry places because they don't need much water.

4. It didn't rain for two months. This caused a _____ and many plants and animals died because they didn't have enough water.

5. Some plants live in dry places and _____ their own water. For example, the saguaro cactus holds water in its skin.

6. People sometimes call the tardigrade a "Moss _____" because it looks like a baby pig.

7. You can find tardigrades on flat land or at the tops of mountains. In fact, they can live at

   both high and low _____.

Expressions

Describing Animal Behavior

Here are some expressions for describing animal behavior:

burns energy	get energy from
has a life span of	live far from
has a heart rate of	have lived for
live in (an environment)	survive in (an environment)

Examples:
Tubeworms <u>live in</u> a stress-free environment.
A shrew <u>has a heart rate of</u> 600 bpm.

Practice

A. Find and underline these expressions decribing animal behavior in "Size and Life Span" or "Extreme Environments."

B. Now use the expressions to complete the following sentences. (Note: *live in* and *survive in* mean about the same thing. You can use either one in the same sentences.)

1. If an animal _____ _____ quickly, it has a fast metabolism.

2. Humans _____ _____ _____ carbohydrates.

3. The average horse _____ _____ _____

_____ _____ 62 years.

4. Tardigrades can _____ _____ any aquatic environment.

5. Some humans _____ _____ _____ over 100 years.

6. It is difficult for many mammals to _____ _____ a very dry environment such as a desert.

7. Some deep-sea fish _____ _____ _____ predators such as sharks.

8. The average polar bear _____ _____ _____

_____ _____ 46 bpm.

Internet Research

Using an Online Science Dictionary

In Chapter 3, you used an online food dictionary. There are many specialized dictionaries on the Internet, including science dictionaries. To find a science word online, go to a science dictionary site such as www.biology_online.org. Type the word that you want to know into the text box. Then click the Search button. Example:

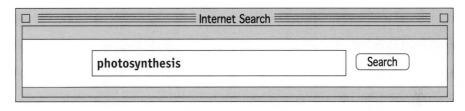

Practice

Look up the following words. Use an online science dictionary such as www.biology_online.org or do a search for "science dictionary" or "biology dictionary."

▶ chromosome
▶ halobacteria
▶ instinct
▶ microhabitat
▶ photosynthesis
▶ plankton
▶ primate
▶ zygote

Then tell the class whether or not you found the word, how you found it, and what it means.

Write About It

A. Write the following paragraphs. Fill in the blanks. Write complete sentences.

Paragraph One

I am/am not very adaptable. Two places I can/cannot survive in are
[Circle one]   [Circle one]

_____ and _____.
        [Write the name of the place]   [Write the name of another place]

I can/cannot survive in _____ because
   [Circle one]   [Write the name of the first place]

_____.
                              [Explain the reason]

Also, I can/cannot survive in _____ because
          [Circle one]   [Write the name of the second place]

_____.
                              [Explain the reason]

Paragraph Two

There are two important things that contribute to longevity in humans. One

is _____. This is important because
        [Give the behavior or habit that contributes to longevity]

_____.
                              [Explain the reason]

Another is _____. This is important because
              [Give another behavior or habit that contributes to longevity]

_____.
                              [Explain the reason]

B. Now write your own paragraphs. First, write one paragraph about being adaptable. Then write another one about habits or behavior that contribute to longevity.

C. Write more paragraphs about animals, longevity, and adaptation. Here are some ideas:
   ▶ Write about an animal that lives in an extreme environment.
   ▶ Write about people who live in an extreme environment such as the Arctic or the desert.

On Your Own

Project

Give a presentation. Do research with a partner. Find information on a living thing (plant, animal, insect, fish) that lives in an extreme environment.

Step 1: Practice

Collect facts about and pictures of your subject. Write notes for your presentation. Use the box below. Practice your presentation with your partner. Have your teacher listen to make sure you are pronouncing words correctly.

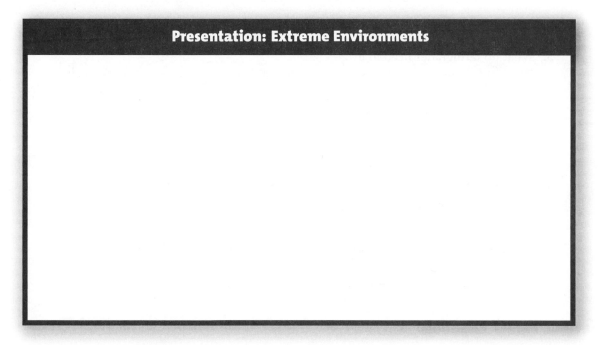

Presentation: Extreme Environments

Step 2: Give a Presentation

Give your presentation to the class with your partner. Take turns speaking. Show your pictures. Make eye contact with (look into the eyes of) your audience. The audience should take notes and ask questions afterwards.

Step 3: Follow-Up

Discuss your presentations. Which were interesting? What made them interesting? What will you do differently the next time that you give a presentation?

Wrap Up

How Much Do You Remember?

Check your new knowledge. In this chapter, you learned facts, words, and expressions. You also learned reading skills and you practiced writing. Complete the following to check what you remember.

1. Why do large animals live longer than small animals?

2. Why might tubeworms live so long?

3. What do tardigrades need to live?

4. Use *survive in* in a sentence.

5. What's another way to preview a reading passage?

6. What word did you find in a science dictionary on the Internet? What does it mean?

Second Timed Readings

Now reread "Size and Life Span" and "Extreme Environments." Time each reading separately. Write your times for all the Timed Readings in this chapter in the Timed Reading Chart on page 215.

Crossword Puzzle

Complete the crossword puzzle to practice some words from this chapter.

CLUES

Across →

1. Tardigrades can _____ _____ very cold places.

5. Tardigrades are _____—they need water to live.

7. The rate at which an organism uses energy

9. A living thing

Down ↓

2. The absence of air

3. A guess

4. Changing appearance and behavior in order to live in a particular environment

6. Poisonous

8. It's in the air that we breathe.

What is Literature?

Literature is poems, short stories, novels and plays that make readers use their imaginations to understand what they are reading. Great literature is the poems, short stories, novels and plays that people continue to think are very good over time. Here are some definitions of these types of literature:

Poetry uses the fewest words to paint a word picture. It uses sound and rhythm. Most poems are meant to be read aloud.

Short stories are usually stories about 5 to 50 pages long.

Novels are longer and usually have more characters than short stories.

Plays are dramatic stories and are meant to be acted.

The *Tale of Genji* is considered to be the world's first full-length novel. A Japanese noblewoman named Murasaki Shikibu in the early eleventh century wrote it.

SOME FAMOUS WRITERS OF LITERATURE

Some famous writers include:

Dante Alighieri—Italian poet, 1265–1321

Miguel de Cervantes—Spanish novelist, 1547–1616

William Shakespeare—English poet and playwright, 1564–1616

Jane Austen—English novelist, 1775–1817

Fyodor Mikhailovich Dostoevsky—Russian novelist, 1821–1881

Marcel Proust—French novelist, 1871–1922

Gabriel García Márquez—Colombian novelist, 1928–

Jin Xuefei (Ha Jin)—Chinese novelist, 1956–

Literature and You

Studying literature is helpful in careers such as teaching, film, advertising, and journalism. It is also helpful in medicine and law. Do you want to study literature? Ask yourself these questions:

- Do I like to read stories?
- Do I like poetry and plays?
- Am I interested in reading stories, poems, and plays carefully?
- Am I curious about characters and why they do what they do?
- Am I interested in reading about different countries and cultures?

Urban Legends

CHAPTER PREVIEW

In this chapter, you'll:

Content
▶ read an urban legend
▶ learn the characteristics of an urban legend

Reading Skills
▶ use titles, headings, topic sentences, and pictures to preview a reading
▶ use context clues to guess the meaning of unknown words

Vocabulary Skills
▶ use words and expressions to talk about urban legends and storytelling
▶ learn more verb + preposition combinations

Writing Skills
▶ write about storytelling and urban legends

Research Skills
▶ combine keywords to find specific urban legends on the Internet
▶ learn people's opinions about telling jokes, stories, and urban legends

The first law of storytelling: Every man is bound to leave a story better than he found it. ❧

—Mrs. Ward Humphrey
(English novelist, 1851–1920)

SHORT SURVEY

I like to listen to:

❑ jokes

❑ anecdotes[1]

❑ rumors[2]

❑ ghost stories

❑ other _____

[1]true stories about people
[2]stories about people, which may or may not be true

Reading 1:
Are there alligators in the sewers of New York? Read "Watch Out for Alligators!" and decide.

Reading 2:
Why do people tell urban legends? Read "The Urban Legend" and find out.

What do you think?

Take the following quiz. Compare your answers with a partner.

What Are You Afraid Of

What are you afraid of? *How* **afraid are you? Circle your answers.**

I'm afraid of:

▶ **Insects, such as bees or spiders**

Extremely   Very   Somewhat   Not at all

▶ **Wild animals, such as bears or alligators**

Extremely   Very   Somewhat   Not at all

▶ **Natural disasters, such as fires or floods**

Extremely   Very   Somewhat   Not at all

▶ **Strange people**

Extremely   Very   Somewhat   Not at all

▶ **Food that will make me sick**

Extremely   Very   Somewhat   Not at all

▶ **Flying in an airplane**

Extremely   Very   Somewhat   Not at all

▶ **Speaking in front of people**

Extremely   Very   Somewhat   Not at all

▶ **Other:** _____

Extremely   Very   Somewhat   Not at all

Now discuss these questions with a partner:
1. What can you do when you are afraid of something? Can people get rid of their fears?
2. Is modern life becoming more and more frightening? Why or why not?

What do you do when you are afraid?

I usually . . .

Reading 1: Watch Out for Alligators!

Before You Read

Preview

A. The title of Reading 1 is "Watch Out for Alligators!" What do you think it's about? Discuss with a partner.

B. Read the following statements. Work with a partner. Do you agree or disagree? Circle your answers.

1. A system for removing wastewater in a city is called a sewer.

    Agree   Disagree

2. Large reptiles, such as alligators, can live in a sewer.

    Agree   Disagree

3. New York City is a very boring place.

    Agree   Disagree

4. New York City is a very scary place.

    Agree   Disagree

5. An alligator's natural habitat is a large city.

    Agree   Disagree

6. Alligators live in Florida.

    Agree   Disagree

7. Alligators are not dangerous.

    Agree   Disagree

8. Alligators make good pets.

    Agree   Disagree

Vocabulary

Preview words and expressions from Reading 1. Complete the sentences below with the correct word or expression from the following box.

> Department of Sanitation   full-grown   go shopping   go sightseeing
> see a play   stay with (someone)   underground   watch out for

1. I want to buy some new clothes. Do you want to _____

   _____ in the city?

2. New York City is famous for its theaters. Should we _____

   _____ _____ when we go there next month?

3. New York City is also famous for its sights, such as the Statue of Liberty and the Empire State

   Building. Do you want to _____ _____ when
   we go there next month?

4. New York City has trains that do not travel above ground. This _____
   transportation system—the subway—is very convenient.

5. My friend lives in New York City. Why don't we _____

   _____ her instead of going to an expensive hotel?

6. New York has a lot of crazy drivers. Please _____

   _____ _____ traffic when you cross
   the streets.

7. Baby alligators can be cute, but _____ alligators are dangerous!

8. My uncle works for the _____ _____

   _____ in a big city. He runs the machines that clean the sewers.

As you read, think about this question:

▶ Is Rafael's story true?

🎧 Watch Out for Alligators!

Linda sent Rafael an email about a trip she is going to take. She is going to New York City. Rafael has some advice for her. Read their emails.

5

#1

From: Linda Yee <lyee@rccc.edu>
Date: Wednesday, April 2, 2008 9:05 PM
To: Rafael Vasquez <rvasquez@rccc.edu>
Subject: Any Advice?

Hi Rafael,

I'm going to New York City for spring break! I'm going to stay with my cousin. I'm so excited! We're going to go sightseeing, shopping, and maybe see a play. You went there last year. What else should I do there? Any advice?

10

Linda

15

#2

From: Rafael Vasquez <rvasquez@rccc.edu>
Date: Wednesday, April 2, 2008 9:30 PM
To: Linda Yee <lyee@rccc.edu>
Subject: Watch Out for Alligators!

Hi Linda,

Hey, that's great! My advice is this: Watch out for alligators!

Rafael

From: Linda Yee <lyee@rccc.edu>
20 Date: Wednesday, April 2, 2008 9:45 PM
To: Rafael Vasquez <rvasquez@rccc.edu>
Subject: Re: Watch Out for Alligators!

What? Are you crazy?

Linda

#3

25 From: Rafael Vasquez <rvasquez@rccc.edu>
Date: Wednesday, April 2, 2008 10:30 PM
To: Linda Yee <lyee@rccc.edu>
Subject: Re: Watch Out for the Alligators!

Hi Linda,

30 No, it's true! There are giant alligators underground in the New York City
sewers. My uncle works for the Department of Sanitation there. A guy that
he works with saw one about a year ago.

I'll tell you why. A long time ago, people used to go to Florida for vacation.
They brought home baby alligators. They brought them home for their kids,
35 as pets. The baby alligators grew. They got mean and ugly. People couldn't
take care of them anymore, so they flushed them down the toilet. Some of
these baby alligators survived in the New York sewer system! They grew and
had babies. Today, there are thousands of full-grown alligators in the
sewers under New York City, so watch out!!

40 Rafael

Word Count: 303

#4

Timed Reading

Read "Watch Out for Alligators!" again. Read
at a comfortable speed. Time your reading.

Start time: _____

End time: _____

My reading time: _____

Comprehension

Fill in the bubble for each correct answer.

1. What is the purpose of Linda's first email (Email #1)?

    (A) to ask a favor   (B) to ask for advice   (C) to ask for some money

2. Who saw the alligator in Rafael's story?

    (A) Rafael   (B) Rafael's uncle   (C) a coworker of Rafael's uncle

3. Rafael might say the story comes from a friend of his uncle because it makes the story seem _____.

    (A) funnier   (B) scarier   (C) truer

4. Rafael's story takes place _____ in a familiar place.

    (A) a long time ago   (B) a few years ago   (C) currently

5. According to the story, how did full-grown alligators get into the sewers in New York City?

    (A) Tourists from Florida brought them to New York.

    (B) People flushed baby alligators down the toilet and they grew there.

    (C) They swam from Florida.

Talk About It

Discuss the following questions:

1. Is this story true? In your opinion, why did Rafael tell it? Why do people tell stories like this?
2. Is this story new to you? If no, talk about the first time that you heard this story. When did you hear it? Who told you the story?

Is the story true?

I think . . .

Reading 2: The Urban Legend

Before You Read

Preview

A. The title of Reading 2 is "The Urban Legend." What do you think it's about? Discuss with a partner.

B. Here are some words and expressions from "The Urban Legend." Use the words to complete the sentences below.

> analyzes   cultures   fable
> feel control over   legend   version

1. Professor Brunvand studies certain types of stories in order to understand them. He wants to know where they come from, how people tell them, and what they mean. He

   _____ these stories and writes books about them.

2. A _____ is an old story from the past, such as the story of Robin Hood. It usually isn't true.

3. Ancient people told stories about nature so that they would be less afraid. Storytelling helped

   them to _____ some _____

   _____ nature.

4. All _____—groups of people with common beliefs and behaviors—
   have stories about their history.

5. There are many ways of telling the story "Watch Out for Alligators!" In one

   _____, the alligators in the sewers are white and cannot see.

6. A _____ is a story that has a lesson. An example is "The Ant and the Grasshopper." The lesson of this story is that it's a good idea to prepare today for difficult times in the future.

Reading Skills

Practice

Answer these questions about "The Urban Legend" on pages 181–182.

1. **Title:** What ideas do you have about the passage from reading the title?

   _____

2. **Headings:** Read the first heading on page 181. What do you think this section is about?

   _____

   Read the second heading on page 181. What do you think this section is about?

   _____

   Read the third heading on page 182. What do you think this section is about?

   _____

3. **Topic Sentences:** Find and read some of the topic sentences. What are the following paragraphs about?

   Paragraph 2: _____

   Paragraph 4: _____

   Paragraph 6: _____

4. **Pictures:** Look at the pictures. Read their captions. What information do they give you about

   the passage? _____

5. Now answer this question: What is "The Urban Legend" probably about?

   (A) background on and examples of urban legends

   (B) specialists who study urban legends

   (C) the history of urban legends

As you read, think about this question:

▶ What are the main characteristics of the urban legend?

🎧 The Urban Legend

> **Storytelling brings back that humanness that we have lost with TV.** 🎤
>
> —*Jackie Torrance,*
> *(African American storyteller,*
> *b. 1944)*

Most modern cultures have urban legends. An urban legend is a story that is strange or hard to believe, and usually it is not true. The person who tells the urban legend *believes* that the story is true. The legend teller helps to make the story sound true in specific ways: The teller says that the story
5 came from a believable source, such as a relative or a friend, or a friend of a friend. Also, the teller might say that the story happened recently, nearby, or in a well-known place.

Urban Legend Characteristics

Urban legends have certain characteristics. An urban legend is similar to a fable. Like a fable, an urban legend usually has a message or a lesson. The lesson often
10 talks about the dangers of modern life, problems with new technology or life in a big city. This is one of the purposes of urban legends—they help people feel more comfortable about things that are new or frightening. Psychologists believe that storytelling is powerful and can help people. For example, when you tell a frightening story, you feel some control over it
15 and a little less afraid. So telling urban legends can help people feel safer. Another characteristic of urban legends is that they change a little every time people retell them.

People usually pass urban legends on to each other orally; that is, they tell them to other people. Also, they tell
20 them in informal language. Recently, the Internet has become another way that they "tell" urban legends: people put them on websites or write them in emails. These urban legends on the Internet are called "netlore."

Some Well-Known Urban Legends

A griot—an African storyteller.

There are many well-known urban legends in America.
25 One is the "Kentucky Fried Rat" story. This story tells of finding a fried rat

instead of fried chicken in a fast-food meal. Another urban legend is "The Vanishing Hitchhiker." This story talks about a hitchhiker. (A hitchhiker is a person who asks strangers for a ride.) The hitchhiker stops a car on a dark road at night and asks the driver for a ride home. When the driver gets to the house, the hitchhiker is gone. The next day, the driver learns that the hitchhiker was a person who died many years ago on that same road.

Some urban legends are very familiar. Many people heard these urban legends when they were growing up. Versions of some of these legends even appear in newspapers, in songs, in movies, and on TV programs. The "Watch Out for Alligators" story is an example of this. A version of this story appeared in a comic book, TV show, and movie. It was called "Teenage Mutant Ninja Turtles." In this version, baby turtles are flushed down the toilet instead of alligators. Unlike the alligators, though, the turtles aren't frightening. They are heroes. Toxic chemicals in the sewer system of a big city change them. These chemicals make them strong. The turtles grow up and use their amazing powers to fight crime in the city.

Urban Legends are Here to Stay

Specialists who study urban legends say these urban stories existed long ago and will remain in the future. One of these specialists is Jan Harold Brunvand. He is a professor at the University of Utah. He collects and analyzes urban legends and writes books about them. According to Brunvand, people will always be telling urban legends. People tell and re-tell urban legends because they like them. Brunvand says that people enjoy telling and hearing stories about danger or strange events, even though they usually know that the stories really aren't true.

Teenage Mutant Ninja Turtles

Word Count: 606

Timed Reading

Read "The Urban Legend" again. Read at a comfortable speed. Time your reading.

Start time: _____

End time: _____

My reading time: _____

After You Read

Main Idea

Which statement best describes the main idea in "The Urban Legend?" Fill in the bubble for the correct answer.

    (A) Most modern cultures have urban legends.

    (B) Urban legends have distinct characteristics and serve an important purpose.

    (C) Some urban legends become television shows.

Getting the Details

Work with a partner. Find information in the reading on the characteristics of urban legends. List at least five characteristics and give an example of or explain each one. The first one is done for you.

Characteristics	Example/Explanation
1. _The story happens in a familiar place._	_"Watch Out for Alligators!" happens in New York City._
2.	
3.	
4.	
5.	

Reading Skills

More Clues for Guessing Meaning from Context

You can often guess the meaning of a new word by looking at its context (the words around it). There are many ways to guess using context. One way is to look for a definition nearby. In Chapter 8, you saw that these definitions often follow certain types of punctuation—such as parentheses and dashes—and certain verbs like *is/are* and *means*. Here are some more examples of clues for finding definitions in context using a word from Chapter 8, *cryptobiosis*.

is/are called	The state in which an animal's metabolism stops <u>is called</u> *cryptobiosis*.
is like	*Cryptobiosis* <u>is like</u> hibernation, but the animal's metabolism completely stops.
that is + explanation	Tardigrades go into *cryptobiosis*. <u>That is</u>, their metabolism stops.

Practice

Use all the clues you know to find definitions (parentheses, dashes, *is/are, means, is/are called, is like,* and *that is* + explanation). Find the following words in "The Urban Legend." Draw a box around each contextual clue. Then write the definition of the word or phrase and the type of contextual clue on the lines.

1. **urban legend:** _____

   Type of contextual clue: _____

2. **orally:** _____

   Type of contextual clue: _____

3. **netlore:** _____

   Type of contextual clue: _____

Vocabulary

A. Here are some words and expressions from in "The Urban Legend." Find them in the reading and circle them.

Nouns	Adjectives	Verb
heroes	believable	fight crime
specialists	specific	

B. Now use the words to complete the sentences.

1. If you say that a story happened to a friend of a friend, it sounds more truthful and

   _____.

2. The Teenage Mutant Ninja Turtles keep people safe because they _____

   _____ in a big city.

3. People who study one thing and are experts at it are called _____.

4. An urban legend has very _____ characteristics such as where it takes place and what it is about; otherwise, it isn't a real urban legend.

5. The _____ of "The Teenage Mutant Turtles" are baby turtles that grow up in the sewers of a big city.

Talk About It

Discuss the following questions:

1. Do you know any urban legends? Tell them to the group.
2. Why do people from all cultures like to tell or listen to stories?

Expressions

More Verb + Preposition Combinations

Here are some more verb + preposition combinations:

  flushed down   put on   pass on (to)   tells about   asks for

Note: You can keep these combinations together or separate them with objects.

Examples:

They <u>flushed</u> *the babies* <u>down</u> the toilet.
They <u>put</u> *these stories* <u>on</u> the Internet.
They <u>pass</u> *these stories* <u>on</u> to their children.
Rafael <u>tells</u> *Linda* <u>about</u> the alligators in the sewers.
The hitchhiker <u>asked</u> *him* <u>for</u> a ride.

Practice

A. Find and underline these verb + preposition expressions in "Watch Out for Alligators!" or "The Urban Legend."

B. Now use them to complete the following sentences.

1. People _____ baby turtles _____ the toilet, and they grew up and became super heroes.

2. The "Kentucky Fried Rat" story _____

   _____ a rat that someone finds in some fried chicken at a fast food restaurant.

3. In "The Vanishing Hitchhiker," a hitchhiker _____ a stranger

   _____ a ride.

4. Rafael likes to _____ urban legends _____ to his friends.

5. If you _____ an urban legend _____ the Internet, it's called "netlore."

Internet Research

Combining Keywords to Find Urban Legends

The Internet is one of the best places to find the latest urban legends. Combining keywords can help you find urban legends on the Internet. For example, if you want information on specific types of urban legends, you can combine a keyword with *urban legend,* such as *alligator.*

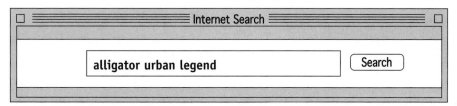

This combination of keywords gives you information about urban legends involving alligators.

Practice

Practice combining keywords with *urban legend* to get specific types of urban legends. Look for the following:

▶ urban legends about alligators
▶ urban legends about fast food
▶ urban legends about microwave ovens
▶ urban legends about technology
▶ urban legends about highways
▶ urban legends about _____ (your topic)

Tell the class about the urban legends that you found and the keyword combinations that you used.

Write About It

A. Write the following paragraphs. Fill in the blanks. Write complete sentences.

Paragraph One

I like/don't like to tell stories for two reasons. One reason is (that) _____
[Circle one]

_____ .
[Explain the reason]

Another reason is (that) _____

_____ .
[Explain the reason]

Paragraph Two

Urban legends have certain characteristics. One characteristic is _____

_____ .
[Describe the characteristic]

For example, _____
[Give an example from an urban legend from this chapter, or another one that you know]

_____ .

Another characteristic is _____ .
[Give another characteristic]

For example, _____ .
[Give another example]

B. Now write your own paragraphs. Write one paragraph about telling stories. Then write another one about the characteristics of the urban legend. Try to include six new words and expressions from this chapter.

C. Write more paragraphs about stories, legends, and urban legends. Here are some ideas:
- ▶ Describe a legend, myth, or fable from any culture.
- ▶ Answer these questions: What is the importance of storytelling? Why do people tell stories? Give examples.

Include six new words or expressions from this chapter in your paragraphs. Also, try to use your Internet research.

On Your Own

Project

Take a survey. Ask your classmates about storytelling.

Step 1: Practice

Listen as your teacher reads the survey questions below. Do you understand them? Repeat the questions with your teacher so you can pronounce them correctly.

Step 2: Take a Survey

Ask three classmates questions about storytelling. Indicate *M* (male) or *F* (female) for each person. Use the form below.

Storytelling Survey

1. Which of these do you like to tell—stories, jokes, urban legends, none of these?

   Person 1 _____ M _____ F Answer: _____

   Person 2 _____ M _____ F Answer: _____

   Person 3 _____ M _____ F Answer: _____

2. Why do you like to tell them or why don't you like to tell them?

   Person 1 Answer: _____

   Person 2 Answer: _____

   Person 3 Answer: _____

3. Tell a story, joke, urban legend, or anecdote.

   Person 1 Answer: _____

   Person 2 Answer: _____

   Person 3 Answer: _____

Step 3: Follow-Up

Explain the results of your survey to the class. For example you could say, "I asked three people about storytelling. Two like to tell jokes and one liked urban legends. Kirk said that he likes to tell jokes. I was surprised because . . . ."

Wrap Up

How Much Do You Remember?

Check your new knowledge. In this chapter, you learned facts, words, and expressions. You also learned reading skills and you practiced writing. Complete the following to check what you remember.

1. What is one characteristic of the urban legend?

   _____

2. Why do people tell urban legends?

   _____

3. What is a *legend*? What is a *fable*?

   _____

4. Use *pass on (to)* in a sentence.

   _____

5. Give an example of a contextual clue.

   _____

6. What combination of keywords might help you find on the Internet urban legends about computers?

   _____

Second Timed Readings

Now reread "Watch Out for Alligators!" and "The Urban Legend." Time each reading separately. Write your times for all the Timed Readings from this chapter in the Timed Reading Chart on page 216.

Crossword Puzzle

Complete the crossword puzzle to practice some words from this chapter.

CLUES

Across ➜
5. If it sounds true, it's _____.
6. Rafael told only one _____ of the alligator story. There are many others.
7. A story from the past that isn't true
8. If you _____ an urban legend _____ the Internet, it becomes "netlore."
9. Where the sewers are

Down ↓
1. A story that has a lesson
2. The alligators in the sewers aren't babies; they're _____-_____.
3. People _____ the baby turtles _____ the toilet.
4. The main characters of a story; they do good things.

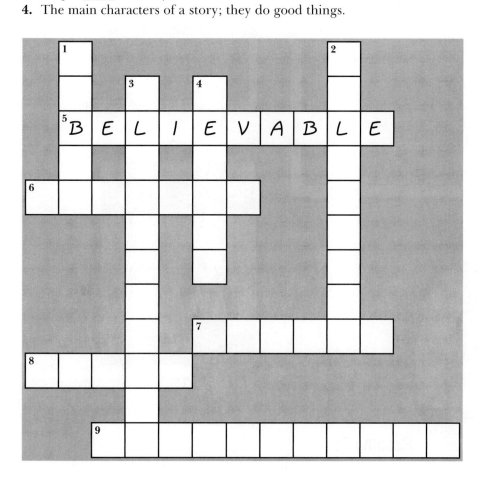

 **Slam Poetry**

CHAPTER PREVIEW

In this chapter, you'll:

Content
▶ read a slam poem
▶ read about slam poetry and slam poetry competitions

Reading Skills
▶ review previewing skills
▶ summarize a reading

Vocabulary Skills
▶ use poetic words and expressions
▶ use words to describe poetry
▶ use verb + *from* and *to* combinations

Writing Skills
▶ compare poems and write a poem

Research Skills
▶ find poems and poets on the Internet
▶ interview people about their favorite poems

> Poetry is all nouns and verbs. 🐌
>
> —*Marianne Moore*
> *(American poet, 1887–1972)*

SHORT SURVEY

I like poems:

❑ about nature

❑ about love

❑ about memories

❑ that don't rhyme

Reading 1:
What is a *slam* poem? Read "Small Boy" to find out.

Reading 2:
What is a *poetry slam*? Read "Slam Poetry" to find out.

What do you think?

Answer the following questions.

Poetry and You

1. Do you like poetry? Why or why not? _____
   _____

2. Why do some people like poetry? _____
   _____

   Why do some people dislike it? _____
   _____

3. Do you know any poems by heart (that you have memorized)? _____

   If yes, which ones?_____

4. Do you know any poems about the following topics?

	Yes	No		Yes	No
baseball	○	○	friendship	○	○
childhood	○	○	love	○	○
dogs	○	○	memories	○	○
failure	○	○	music	○	○
family	○	○	success	○	○
flowers	○	○	trees	○	○

5. Have you ever written a poem? _____ If yes, what was it about? _____

   If no, could you write a poem? _____ If yes, about what?

Compare your answers with a partner.

Reading 1: Small Boy

Before You Read

Preview

A. The title of Reading 1 is "Small Boy." What do you think it's about? Discuss with a partner.

B. You are going to read a poem. The poet—a person who writes a poem—writes about the past, when he was a small (young) boy. Work with a partner. Make some guesses about the poem. Write your guesses on the lines after the questions.

1. Do you think the poem "Small Boy" is about happy memories or sad memories?

_____

2. Where do young boys usually like to play?

_____

3. What kinds of things do small boys like to do?

_____

4. Who are the important people in a young boy's life?

_____

5. What do children like to do in the rain?

_____

6. How do children feel about storms?

_____

7. What do children like to do with autumn leaves?

_____

8. What are children's senses (hearing, feeling, seeing, tasting, and smelling) usually like? Are they strong or weak?

_____

Vocabulary

Preview these words from Reading 1. Fill in the bubble for each correct answer.

1. What are *footsteps*?

(A) Footsteps are the steps in front of a house.

(B) Footsteps are the steps that people make when they walk.

(C) Footsteps are the first steps that a baby takes.

2. What is *a moment*?

(A) It is a part of a poem.

(B) It is a memory from long ago.

(C) It is a short time, less than one minute.

3. What is an *empire*?

(A) land usually ruled by a king or queen

(B) clothing with gold and silver

(C) metal, very shiny and clean

4. What is *thunder*?

(A) the smell during a rainstorm

(B) the light during a rainstorm

(C) the noise during a rainstorm

5. What is *lightening*?

(A) the cold air that you sometimes feel during a storm

(B) the flash of light that you sometimes see during a storm

(C) the noise that you sometimes hear during a storm

As you read, think about this question:
▶ Are the poet's memories happy or sad?

> The essentials of poetry are rhythm, dance and the human voice. 🖎
>
> —*Earle Birney*
> *(Canadian poet, 1904–1995)*

🎧 Small Boy

Marc Smith is the father of Slam Poetry. He wrote and performed the following poem, titled "Small Boy." The poem comes from early childhood memories of playing on the lawn in the summer. Here is how the poem begins and ends:

> These were the footsteps.
> Someone was coming.
> No one to listen.
> No one to care.
>
> He was a small boy
> Running from father.
> He was a father
> Running to son.
>
> They were a moment
> Caught in a photo.
> Caught in the sunlight.
> Caught in a spin.
>
> Here is the green lawn
> Under the sunlight.
> Green is the empire
> Bounded by walks.

Here he is running
Fast through the red leaves
25 Falling in autumn
Into a pile.
* * * * * *

He was a small boy
Running from father.
He was a father
30 Running to son.

They were a moment
Caught in a photo.
Caught in the sunlight.
Caught in a spin.

35 This was the rain.
This was the thunder.
This was the lightning
Stitching the sky.

This was the bright blue.
40 This was the sunlight.
These are the stars
Spinning on high.

Word Count: 179

Timed Reading

Read "Small Boy" again. Read at a comfortable speed. Time your reading.

Start time: _____

End time: _____

My reading time: _____

After You Read

Comprehension

A. Are the poet's memories happy or sad? Circle your answer.

Happy Sad

B. Fill in the bubble for each correct answer.

1. The first line of the poem talks about footsteps. Whose footsteps is it talking about?

 Ⓐ the boy's   Ⓑ the father's Ⓒ the mother's

2. Why is the boy running?

 Ⓐ Because no one took his photo.

 Ⓑ Because no one saw him.

 Ⓒ Because no one was listening to him.

3. The introduction tells you which season the poet is writing about. What season is it?

 Ⓐ summer   Ⓑ winter   Ⓒ autumn

4. Another season is mentioned in the poem. What season is it?

 Ⓐ summer   Ⓑ winter   Ⓒ autumn

5. Where is the boy playing?

 Ⓐ on the sidewalk Ⓑ on the lawn Ⓒ in the garden

Talk About It

First, read the poem out loud. Then discuss the following questions:

1. When you read the poem out loud, did it sound sad? Why or why not?

2. Poetry makes images in your mind. What images do you see as you read the poem?

3. What is your favorite childhood memory?

Reading 2: Slam Poetry

Before You Read

Preview

A. The title of Reading 2 is "Slam Poetry." What do you think it's about? Discuss with a partner.

B. Preview these words from the reading. Complete each sentence below with the correct word.

> | | | | |
> |---|---|---|---|
> | bang | competition | construction | dramatic |
> | judge | national | organized | rage |

1. The poet felt strong anger, so he wrote a poem about his _____.

2. People came to the poetry contest from all over the country. There were teams from every

   state at this _____ contest.

3. Jane loves to write poetry. Poets don't make a lot of money, so Jane makes money by helping

   to build houses. She's a _____worker.

4. The school had a poetry contest. Ron wrote a poem for the contest and was very excited to

   learn that he won the _____.

5. The poet wrote about the loud noise of a gun, so he wrote the word

   "_____" in his poem.

6. Wilson's life was not dull; it was very exciting and emotional. Therefore, his poetry was very

   _____.

7. Marti had to decide which poem was the best. She was the _____ for the
   poetry contest.

8. Marc Smith found a large room and invited poets to the first contest that he

   _____ in 1987.

Reading Skills

Combine Skills to Preview a Reading

In previous chapters, you used titles, headings, pictures and captions, introductions, and topic sentences to preview a reading passage. You can use all of these strategies together. You can also use only the ones that work best for you.

Practice

A. Preview "Slam Poetry" on pages 201–202. Use any or all of the previewing strategies. Take notes.

> **Notes:**
>
> *Title: "Slam Poetry"*
> _____
>
> _____
>
> _____
>
> _____
>
> _____
>
> _____
>
> _____
>
> _____
>
> _____

B. Discuss the following questions:
1. What is the main idea of "Slam Poetry?" How do you know?
2. What are some of the supporting ideas? How do you know?
3. Which previewing strategies did you use? Why did you use these?

What is the main idea?

I think it's . . .

As you read, think about this question:
▶ What is slam poetry?

🎧 Slam Poetry

Most cultures have poems. People told poems to one another thousands of years ago. In China, poems go back to the Zhou Dynasty (1125–225 B.C.). Mayan poetry dates back to the fifth century A.D., and the Greeks had their poets, too. The ancient Greeks read poems such as the *Iliad* and *Odyssey* aloud over several
5   days. The *Iliad* and *Odyssey* are still popular today, but now people read them in books.

What is Slam Poetry?

A new form of poetry, called "slam poetry," started in Chicago in 1987. Slam poetry is not only oral, but it's also competitive. People perform slam poetry at competitions. The poet memorizes the poem and tells it to the audience. Slam
10   poets rarely read from a piece of paper. Slam poetry is also very dramatic. It makes the audience react strongly. For instance, the audience may shout and yell at slam competitions. The poet may also walk into the audience or start singing.

The father of slam poetry is Marc Smith. He was a construction worker. He started a poetry-reading series at a lounge in Chicago in 1984. Then, in 1987, he
15   organized the first slam competition at the Green Mill Jazz Club in Chicago. Slam poetry competitions continue every week at the Green Mill Jazz Club. The first national slam took place in 1990 in San Francisco, with four-person teams from Chicago, San Francisco, and New York.

Characteristics of Slam Poetry

Slam poetry is like other poetry. It has a lot of ideas and thoughts. The topics
20   of slam poetry usually have to do with feelings. These feelings can be rage, despair, terror, sadness, or other emotions. Slam poetry has a strong beat. For example, there is a lot of stress on important words. The poet expresses thoughts sharply—bang, bang, bang. Some of the poems rhyme and others do not.

Slam Poetry Competitions

At a slam poetry competition, a slam poet usually has three minutes to perform a poem. The poet tries to speak for all three minutes, but does not want to go over the time limit. There is a ten-second grace period (extra time that doesn't count). After the ten extra seconds, the poet loses points for going too long. Members of the audience are the judges. They rate the poems from 0.0 to10.0. Just like competitive sports, slam poetry has a season. The slam season is from September to April.

Slam poets are very competitive, but they also believe that the poetry is more important than winning. The slam poet Allan Wolf once said, "The points are not the point, the point is the poetry." Now over 45 teams compete in slams. Over 3,000 people attend the national competition each year.

Word Count: 455

Timed Reading

Read "Slam Poetry" again. Read at a comfortable speed. Time your reading.

Start time: _____

End time: _____

My reading time: _____

After You Read

Main Idea

Which statement best describes the main idea of "Slam Poetry"? Fill in the bubble for the correct answer.

(A) A large number of people attend slam poetry contests every year.

(B) Most cultures have poems that are over 1,000 years old.

(C) Slam poetry is a new form of poetry.

Getting the Details

Fill in the following chart with characteristics of slam poets, slam poet audiences, slam poetry, and slam poetry competitions.

	Characteristics
Slam poets	
Slam poet audiences	
Slam poems	
Slam poetry competitions	

Reading Skills

Summarizing

A summary is a short description of a reading passage. You include the main ideas of the passage, but you write them in your own words.

A summary has certain characteristics:
- ▶ it is shorter than the original passage
- ▶ it tells only the main ideas
- ▶ it does not give much detailed information
- ▶ it does not give opinions about the passage
- ▶ it mentions the title and/or the author of the passage

Writing a summary is a good way to take notes on and remember reading passages. Summaries also help you take tests and write papers.

Here is a summary of "The Urban Legend":

> The article, "The Urban Legend", defines and describes the characteristics of the urban legend and gives some examples. An urban legend is a story that isn't true. People pass on urban legends orally, and they change them slightly each time they tell them. The teller seems to believe the story, and makes it more believable by placing it in a familiar location and by saying that the story happened to a friend or a friend of a friend. Urban legends often teach lessons about modern life such as dealing with new technology or living in a big city. Some well-known American urban legends are "Alligators in the Sewer" and "The Vanishing Hitchhiker."

To write a summary:
- ▶ Reread the article.
- ▶ Take notes as you read. Put the main ideas into your own words.
- ▶ Reread what you wrote. Make sure you have only the main ideas. Make sure you don't include opinions.
- ▶ Revise if necessary.

Practice

Write a summary of "Slam Poetry" on a separate piece of paper. Compare your summary with a partner. Answer the following questions about your partner's summary:
1. How long is the summary?
2. Did your partner include all the main ideas and *only* main ideas?
3. Does the summary mention the title of the passage?
4. Is there any information that should not be in the summary? Is there any information missing from the summary?

Vocabulary

A. Here are some more words and expressions from "Slam Poetry." Find them in the reading and circle them.

Nouns	Verbs	Adjective
despair grace period terror	expresses rate	Mayan

B. Now use them to complete the sentences below.

1. Like people from many cultures, the _____ people enjoyed poetry. This ancient culture lived in what is now Central America.

2. The poetry slam had a time limit of only two minutes, but Joe's poem took two and a half minutes. This was O.K. because there was a _____ _____ of 30 seconds.

3. Because Ken was very afraid of the dark, many of his poems were about night

   _____ .

4. Some people say what they want to say in paintings; others say things with music. Beth

   _____ her thoughts with poetry.

5. Louise felt great sadness. She wrote about her _____ in her poem "No One To Love."

6. Poetry slam judges give points to poems. They _____ them on things such as subject, performance, and timing.

Talk About It

Discuss the following questions:
Would you like to read poetry at a poetry slam? Why or why not?

Would you like to read poetry at a poetry slam?

Yes, I think . . .

Expressions

Verbs with *to* and *from*

Here are some verbs with *to* and *from*:

dates back to	rate . . . from . . . to . . .	running from
go back to	read from	running to

Examples: The poem <u>dates back to</u> Mayan times.
The poems <u>go back to</u> the Zhou Dynasty
The judges <u>rate</u> the poems <u>from</u> 1 <u>to</u> 10.
Slam poets memorize their poems; they don't <u>read from</u> a piece of paper.
First I saw him <u>running from</u> his father and then I saw him <u>running to</u> his father.

Notes: *From* shows the source.
To shows the direction.
Both *date back to* and *go back to* are time expressions.

Practice

A. Find and underline the verbs with *to* and *from* in the box in "Small Boy" or "Slam Poetry."

B. Now use them to complete the following sentences.

1. The small boy had a frightening dream. A monster was chasing him. The boy was

   _____ _____ the monster, but he fell.

2. The soccer player was _____ _____ the goal. He kicked the ball and got a point for his team.

3. I like to _____ _____ Robert Frost's book of poems before I go to sleep.

4. My first poem _____ _____ _____ 1990. I wrote it when I was 10 years old.

5. In this competition, the judges _____ _____ 1 _____ 20; Joe's poem got a 20, the highest score.

6. This old English poem _____ _____ _____ 1100 A.D.

Internet Research

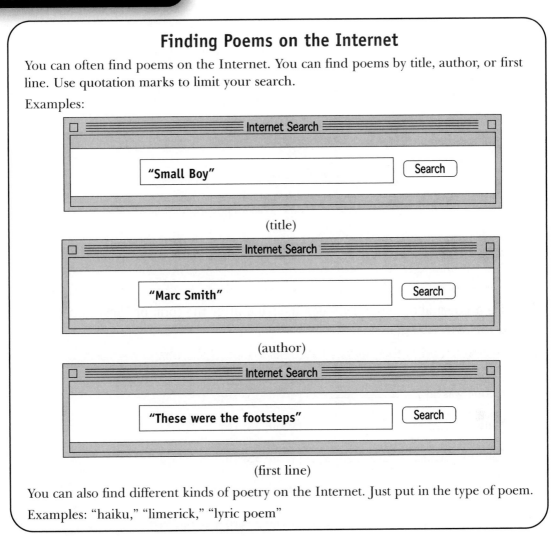

Finding Poems on the Internet

You can often find poems on the Internet. You can find poems by title, author, or first line. Use quotation marks to limit your search.

Examples:

Internet Search
"Small Boy" [Search]

(title)

Internet Search
"Marc Smith" [Search]

(author)

Internet Search
"These were the footsteps" [Search]

(first line)

You can also find different kinds of poetry on the Internet. Just put in the type of poem.

Examples: "haiku," "limerick," "lyric poem"

Practice

Find a poem on the Internet. Use the title or the first line. Print the results. Then use a search engine or a biography site and look up the poet. Bring the results to class and talk about the poet. Read the poem to your classmates.

Here are some famous American poets: Emily Dickinson, Langston Hughes, Marianne Moore, Edgar Allan Poe, Carl Sandburg, Walt Whitman, Philip Levine, Allen Ginsberg, and Rita Dove. Use one of them, or a poet from any culture or country.

Then try looking for another kind of poetry, for example, haiku or limerick.

Write About It

Paragraph

Write the following paragraph. Fill in the spaces. Write complete sentences.

My favorite poem is _____ by
[Give the name of the poem]

_____. I like this poem because _____
[Give the name of the author]

_____ .
[Explain one reason why you like the poem]

I also like it because _____
[Explain another reason why you like the poem]

_____ .

Poem

A. Write a poem about your own idea modeled after the form of "Small Boy." Fill in the blanks. Write complete sentences.

There were the _____ [Write a noun]

Someone was _____ [Write a verb]

No one to _____ [Write a verb]

No one to _____ [Write a verb]

He was _____ [Write an article, an adjective, and a noun]

_____ [Write a verb + *to* or *from*]

B. Now write your own paragraph and poem. First, write a paragraph about a poem that you like. Try to include six new words and expressions from this chapter. Then write a poem like "Small Boy" about childhood memories or nature.

C. Write more paragraphs about poetry or write another poem. Here are some ideas:
▶ Write about the poem or the poet that you found on the Internet.
▶ Write about why people write poems.
▶ Write a slam poem. Make it short. Make it express strong feelings.

On Your Own

Project

Take a survey. Ask your classmates about their favorite poems.

Step 1: Practice

Listen as your teacher reads the survey questions below. Do you understand them? Repeat the questions with your teacher so you can pronounce them correctly.

Step 2: Take a Survey

Ask three classmates about their favorite poems. Indicate M (male) or F (female) for each person. Use the form below.

Poetry Survey

1. What is your favorite poem? Who is the author?

   Person 1 _____ M _____ F   Answer: _____

   Person 2 _____ M _____ F   Answer: _____

   Person 3 _____ M _____ F   Answer: _____

2. When was the poem written? What is it about?

   Person 1   Answer: _____

   Person 2   Answer: _____

   Person 3   Answer: _____

3. What do you know about the author? Why do you think that he or she wrote this poem?

   Person 1   Answer: _____

   Person 2   Answer: _____

   Person 3   Answer: _____

Step 3: Follow-Up

Explain the results of your survey to the class. For example you might say, "I asked three people about their favorite poems... Two people liked..."

Wrap Up

How Much Do You Remember?

Check your new knowledge. In this chapter you learned facts, words, and expressions. You also learned reading skills and you practiced writing. Complete the following to check what you remember.

1. What is a slam poem?

   _____

2. What are the rules of a slam poetry competition?

   _____

3. Who invented slam poetry?

   _____

4. Use *organized* in a sentence.

   _____

5. Use this expression in a sentence: *dates back to*.

   _____

6. What are the characteristics of a summary?

   _____

Second Timed Readings

Now reread "Small Boy" and "Slam Poetry." Time each reading separately. Write your times for all Timed Readings in this chapter in the Timed Reading Chart on page 216.

Crossword Puzzle

Complete the crossword puzzle to practice some words from this chapter.

CLUES

Across →
5. The noise that a gun makes
6. An ancient culture in Mexico
7. A short time, less than a minute
8. He _____ his feelings in his poems.
9. Great sadness

Down ↓
1. Light during a rainstorm
2. Noise during a rainstorm
3. Great anger
4. Extra time that doesn't count

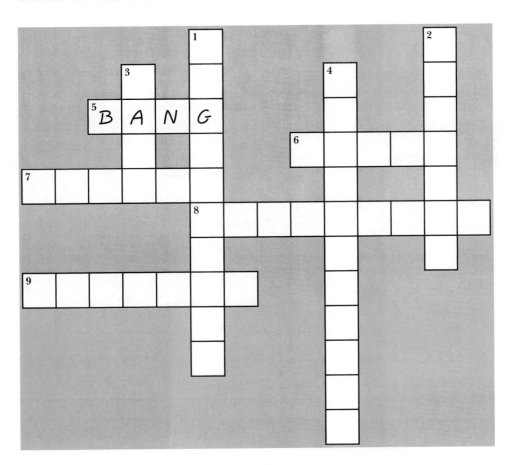

Timed Reading Chart

Use this chart to keep track of your reading times.

UNIT 1 Psychology

CHAPTER 1: Friendship

Can You Do Me a Favor?
Page 8

First Reading

Start time: _____

End time: _____

My reading time: _____

Second Reading

Start time: _____

End time: _____

My reading time: _____

The Benefits of Friendship
Page 13

First Reading

Start time: _____

End time: _____

My reading time: _____

Second Reading

Start time: _____

End time: _____

My reading time: _____

CHAPTER 2: Finding Lost Loves

Lost Loves: One Couple's Story
Page 28

First Reading

Start time: _____

End time: _____

My reading time: _____

Second Reading

Start time:

End time:

My reading time: _____

The Lost Love Study
Page 33

First Reading

Start time: _____

End time: _____

My reading time: _____

Second Reading

Start time: _____

End time: _____

My reading time: _____

UNIT ② Food and Nutrition

CHAPTER 3: Food Names

Soup du Jour
Page 50

First Reading

Start time: _____

End time: _____

My reading time: _____

Second Reading

Start time: _____

End time: _____

My reading time: _____

The Language of Food
Page 55

First Reading

Start time: _____

End time: _____

My reading time: _____

Second Reading

Start time: _____

End time: _____

My reading time: _____

CHAPTER 4: Food and Health

Nutrition "Dos and Don'ts" for 5,200 Years
Page 70

First Reading

Start time: _____

End time: _____

My reading time: _____

Second Reading

Start time: _____

End time: _____

My reading time: _____

Foods That are Good for You
Page 75

First Reading

Start time: _____

End time: _____

My reading time: _____

Second Reading

Start time: _____

End time: _____

My reading time: _____

Timed Reading Chart

Use this chart to keep track of your reading times.

CHAPTER 5: The Physics of Sports

Sports Q & A		Page 92
First Reading	**Second Reading**	
Start time: _____	Start time: _____	
End time: _____	End time: _____	
My reading time: _____	My reading time: _____	

Athletes and the Laws of Physics		Page 97
First Reading	**Second Reading**	
Start time: _____	Start time: _____	
End time: _____	End time: _____	
My reading time: _____	My reading time: _____	

CHAPTER 6: Sports History

The First Mile Under Four Minutes		Page 112
First Reading	**Second Reading**	
Start time: _____	Start time: _____	
End time: _____	End time: _____	
My reading time: _____	My reading time: _____	

Sports and History		Page 117
First Reading	**Second Reading**	
Start time: _____	Start time: _____	
End time: _____	End time: _____	
My reading time: _____	My reading time: _____	

CHAPTER 7: Nature or Nurture?

Twins: Separated at Birth   **Page 134**
First Reading   **Second Reading**

Start time: _____   Start time: _____

End time: _____   End time: _____

My reading time: _____   My reading time: _____

Nature *and* Nurture   **Page 139**
First Reading   **Second Reading**

Start time: _____   Start time: _____

End time: _____   End time: _____

My reading time: _____   My reading time: _____

CHAPTER 8: Oddities in Living Nature

Size and Life Span   **Page 154**
First Reading   **Second Reading**

Start time: _____   Start time: _____

End time: _____   End time: _____

My reading time: _____   My reading time: _____

Extreme Environments   **Page 159**
First Reading   **Second Reading**

Start time: _____   Start time: _____

End time: _____   End time: _____

My reading time: _____   My reading time: _____

Timed Reading Chart

Use this chart to keep track of your reading times.

UNIT 5 Literature

CHAPTER 9: Urban Legends

Watch Out for Alligators!   **Page 176**
First Reading   **Second Reading**

Start time: _____   Start time: _____

End time: _____   End time: _____

My reading time: _____   My reading time: _____

The Urban Legend   **Page 181**
First Reading   **Second Reading**

Start time: _____   Start time: _____

End time: _____   End time: _____

My reading time: _____   My reading time: _____

CHAPTER 10: Slam Poetry

Small Boy   **Page 196**
First Reading   **Second Reading**

Start time: _____   Start time: _____

End time: _____   End time: _____

My reading time: _____   My reading time: _____

Slam Poetry   **Page 201**
First Reading   **Second Reading**

Start time: _____   Start time: _____

End time: _____   End time: _____

My reading time: _____   My reading time: _____

Vocabulary Index

Chapter 1

are better than
benefits
come over
do a favor for
do volunteer work
emotional
feel less stress
help each other
is more difficult than
live longer
live near each other
makes people healthier than
material
mentally
patients
pay (me) back
physically
pick (it) up
political ideas
recover sooner than
recovered
researchers
save the environment
scientific studies
see each other
send emails to each other

Chapter 2

adore
be crazy about
be fond of
be in love with
be mad about
break up
care for
collected information from
come back
concluded (something)
conducted an interview
end in
fall in love
get married
go away
human emotions
included
interested in

is/was interested in
learned (something) about
like
lost love
love
participant
partner
received information
reconnected
renew their relationship
result in
separate
soul mate
talked about
wondered about
worship

Chapter 3

ask for
burrito
croissant
depending on
dim sum
expensive
forget about
invented
look at
match
Midwest
mixed with
pad thai
pizza
popular
renamed
sushi

Chapter 4

ancient
antioxidants
arthritis
beneficial
brittle
cancer
carbohydrates
compounds
conquered
corpulence

cured
fever
flu
folk medicine
headache
inflammation
nutrition
prescribes X for Y
reduced
reincarnation
sore throat
superstitions
timid
to fast
traditional medicine
tumor
use X for Y
vegetarian
X cures/cured Y
X might prevent Y
X keeps / can keep you well / healthy
X helps to heal Y
X is used for Y
X is used to treat Y

Chapter 5

arrow
backboard
bat
bathing cap
bow
curb
equally
force
go as fast (as)
go headfirst
go higher (than)
goes farther (than)
goes faster (than)
goes in the direction of
golf club
grams
ground
hockey stick
home plate
hoop
in motion
lane dividers

MPH
mud
object
puck
racquet
resists
right field
tee
tennis ball

Chapter 6

ahead of
at + age
break the record
chased
crosswind
economist
extremely
flat
in + period of time
inventor
mechanics
missionary
musician
myths
no different from
on + specific date
philosopher
printer
religious
rope
scientist
skulls
track
training

Chapter 7

adopt
affect
appearance
(be) born with
(be) separated at birth
candidates
combination (of heredity and environment)
debate
develop after
develop from
DNA
environment

fraternal twins
genes
heredity
identical twins
IQ
overcomes
reunited
share the same DNA
siblings
standardized
training
versus

Chapter 8

adaptation
altitudes
approximate
(be) an exception
biologists
burns energy
carbon dioxide
drought
flexible
get energy from
has a heart rate of
has a lifespan of
have lived for
hold their breath
hypothesis
life span
live far from
live in (an environment)
mammals
metabolism
multi-celled
organism
oxygen
piglet
rate
segments
species
store
survive
survive in (an environment)
ultraviolet light
vacuum

Chapter 9

analyzes
asks for

believable
cultures
Department of Sanitation
fable
feel control over
fight crime
flushed down
full-grown
go shopping
go sightseeing
heroes
legend
pass on (to)
put on
see a play
specialists
specific
stay with (someone)
tells about
underground
version
watch out for

Chapter 10

bang
competition
construction
dates back to
despair
dramatic
empire
expresses
footsteps
go back to
grace period
judge
lightning
Mayan
moment
national
organized
rage
rate
rate ... from ... to ....
read from
running from
running to
terror
thunder

Skills Index

Text Credits

p. 49–50 "Metropolitan Diary" by Joe Rogers in The New York Times, February 10, 2003. Copyright © 2003 by The New York Times Co. Reprinted with permission.

p. 196–197 "Small Boy" first appeared in Crowdpleaser, Collage Press, 1996. Copyright © 1996, 2000 by Marc Smith. All rights reserved. Reprinted with permission of Marc K. Smith.

Crossword puzzles were created using Crossword Express from AUS-PC_SOFT (www.crAUSwords.com).

Photo Credits

From the Getty Images Royalty-Free Collection: p. 2; p. 4, left; p. 4, right; p. 6; p. 13; p. 14; p. 24, left; p. 26, top; p. 26, bottom; p. 32; p. 46, left; p. 46, right; p. 50; p. 54, photo a; p. 54, photo b; p. 54, photo c; p. 54, photo d; p. 55; p. 66, left; p. 66, right; p. 70; p. 75, top; p. 75, bottom; p. 86; p. 88, top; p. 88, bottom; p. 90, photo 1; p. 90, photo 2; p. 90, photo 4; p. 92, top left; p. 92, bottom; p. 97, middle; p. 97, bottom; p. 98; p. 108, right; p. 116, left; p. 116, right; p. 117, top; p. 117, bottom; p. 118, middle; p. 118, bottom; p. 128; p. 133, left; p. 133, right; p. 150, left; p. 150, right; p. 152, middle; p. 152, right; p. 154, left; p. 159; p. 172, right; p. 174; p. 192, right; p. 194; p. 196, top; p. 196, bottom.

From the CORBIS Royalty-Free Collection: cover, top left; cover, top right; cover, bottom right; p. 24, right; p. 28; p. 44, p. 133, middle; p. 170.

Other Images: cover, bottom left: Gary Conner/PhotoEdit; p. 33: Erik Dreyer/Getty Images; p. 90, photo 3: Digital Vision/Getty Images; p. 92, top right: Digital Vision/Getty Images; p. 95: Digital Vision/Getty Images; p. 97, top: Bettmann/CORBIS ; p. 108, left: CORBIS ; p. 112: CORBIS ; p. 118, top: Bettmann/CORBIS; p. 130, left: Photo courtesy of New York City plastic surgeon Dr. Darrick E. Antell; p. 130, right: Thomas Wanstall/The Image Works; p. 134: Thomas Wanstall/The Image Works; p. 140, left: Photo courtesy of New York City plastic surgeon Dr. Darrick E. Antell; p. 140, right: Photo courtesy of New York City plastic surgeon Dr. Darrick E. Antell; p. 152, left: Docwhite/Getty Images; p. 154, right: Dr. Carleton Ray/Photo Researchers, Inc.; p. 160: Carolina Biological/Getty Images; p. 172, left: Gideon Mendel/CORBIS; p. 181: Anthony Bannister; Gallo Images/CORBIS; p. 182: CORBIS SYGMA; p. 192, left: Kevin Fleming/CORBIS; p. 202: Kevin Fleming/CORBIS.